Easy Cakes

Easy Cakes

This edition first published in 1989
exclusively for Marks and Spencer p.l.c.
by arrangement with
the Octopus Publishing Group
Michelin House, 81 Fulham Road
London SW3 6RB
© Hennerwood Publications Limited, 1989
ISBN 0 86273 537 8
Printed in Spain by Imprenta Hispano-Americana, Barcelona

Contents

Everyday cakes

◆

Despite the proliferation of packaged cake mixes
and the easy availability of baked goods in shops
and supermarkets, there are still a great many
cake makers around, who take much pleasure from
baking for their family and friends.
Cakes to be enjoyed everyday are by no means
plain, but are ideal for serving with tea or coffee.
Several of the cakes in this chapter can also be
served hot as a pudding.
The cake recipes here contain fresh fruit as well as
glacé, candied and dried fruits, coconut, and lots
of different kinds of nuts. Many are iced – with
buttercream, glacé icing or a glossy meringue-type
frosting – and one has a crumble topping.

Iced Walnut Cake (see recipe on page 8).

ICED WALNUT CAKE

175g (6oz) butter, softened
175g (6oz) light soft brown sugar or caster sugar
3 eggs
175g (6oz) self-raising flour, sifted
1 tablespoon black treacle
50g (2oz) shelled walnuts, chopped
walnut halves, to decorate
ICING:
150g (5oz) caster sugar
1 egg white
1 tablespoon water
1 tablespoon coffee essence or very strong black coffee
a good pinch of cream of tartar

Preparation time: 40 minutes
Cooking time: 45–50 minutes
Oven: 180°C, 350°F, Gas Mark 4

1. Grease a 20cm (8 inch) round cake tin and line with greased greaseproof paper.
2. Cream the butter and sugar together until light and fluffy and pale in colour. Beat in the eggs one at a time following each with a spoonful of flour.
3. Fold in the remaining flour, followed by the black treacle and walnuts. Turn into the prepared tin and level the top.
4. Bake in a preheated oven for 45–50 minutes or until well risen, golden brown and just firm to the touch. Turn out on to a wire rack and leave until cold; then strip off the paper.
5. For the icing: put all the ingredients into a heatproof bowl set over a saucepan of gently simmering water. Stir until the sugar has dissolved, then whisk well with a hand-held electric mixer or balloon whisk, scraping down the sides of the bowl fairly frequently, until the mixture stands in fairly stiff peaks.
6. Spread the icing quickly and evenly over the whole cake using a round-bladed knife to swirl it attractively. Decorate with walnut halves and leave to set.

Makes a 20cm (8 inch) round cake (8 slices)

Nutrition content per serving   Carbohydrate: 62g   Fat: 24g
Fibre: 1g   Kilocalories: 469

COFFEE BUTTERMILK CAKE

175g (6oz) self-raising flour
150g (5oz) caster sugar
5 tablespoons vegetable oil
4 tablespoons buttermilk
1 tablespoon coffee essence or strong black coffee
2 eggs, separated
chocolate crisp wafers or biscuits, to decorate
BUTTERCREAM:
75g (3oz) butter, preferably unsalted
1 egg yolk
225g (8oz) icing sugar, sifted
a few drops of vanilla essence
a little milk

Preparation time: 30 minutes
Cooking time: 30 minutes
Oven: 180°C, 350°F, Gas Mark 4

1. Grease two 18cm (7 inch) sandwich tins and line the bottoms with greased greaseproof paper.
2. Sift the flour into a bowl, add the sugar and mix well.
3. Add the oil, buttermilk, coffee essence or coffee and egg yolks and beat well until smooth: about 2 minutes with an electric mixer or 3 minutes if mixing by hand.
4. Whisk the egg whites until stiff and fold evenly through the mixture. Pour into the tins and level the tops.
5. Place in a preheated oven and bake for 25–30 minutes or until well risen and firm to the touch. Turn out on to a wire rack and leave until cold.
6. For the buttercream, melt the butter in a pan. Remove from the heat and gradually beat in the egg yolk and icing sugar with the vanilla essence and sufficient milk to give a light spreading consistency.
7. Use about a third of the buttercream to sandwich the cakes together and a further third to spread over the top. Put the remainder into a piping bag fitted with a star nozzle.
8. Arrange the chocolate crisp wafers or biscuits in a wheel design over the top of the cake with piped stars of buttercream to hold them in position.

Makes an 18cm (7 inch) round sandwich cake (8 slices)

Nutrition content per serving   Carbohydrate: 72g   Fat: 22g
Fibre: 1g   Kilocalories: 487

Coffee Buttermilk Cake.

DARK GINGER CAKE

175g (6oz) black treacle
40g (1½oz) demerara sugar
75g (3oz) butter
175g (6oz) plain flour
2 teaspoons ground ginger
1 teaspoon ground mixed spice
½ teaspoon bicarbonate of soda
2 eggs
100ml (4fl oz) milk or buttermilk
a few pieces of stem or crystallized ginger
GINGER BUTTERCREAM:
2 egg yolks
75g (3oz) caster sugar
4 tablespoons water
175g (6oz) butter
pinch of ground ginger or mixed spice

Preparation time: 45 minutes, plus standing and 24 hours storing
Cooking time: about 1¼ hours
Oven: 160°C, 325°F, Gas Mark 3

1. Grease a 23 × 13cm (9 × 5 inch) loaf tin and line with greased greaseproof paper.
2. Put the treacle, sugar and butter into a pan and heat gently until melted, then cool slightly.
3. Sift the flour, ginger, spice and bicarbonate of soda into a bowl and make a well in the centre.
4. Add the eggs, milk or buttermilk and the melted treacle mixture and beat until smooth.
5. Pour into the tin, place in a preheated oven and bake for about 1¼ hours or until a skewer inserted in the centre comes out clean.
6. Turn out on to a wire rack and leave until cold; then wrap in foil and store for at least 24 hours before eating.
7. For the buttercream, beat the egg yolks in a bowl until smooth. Put the sugar and water into a pan and heat gently until the sugar dissolves, then boil steadily until the syrup reaches 107°C (225°F) on a sugar thermometer.
8. Remove from the heat and immediately pour on to the egg yolks, whisking well all the time. Continue to whisk until very light and fluffy.
9. Cream the butter until soft and gradually beat in the egg and sugar mixture. Flavour with a pinch of ground ginger or spice and spread or pipe over the top of the cake. Decorate with pieces of ginger.

Makes a 23 × 13cm (9 × 5 inch) loaf cake (12 slices)

Nutrition content per serving   Carbohydrate: 34g   Fat: 20g
Fibre: 1g   Kilocalories: 317

GLACE CHERRY CAKE

225g (8oz) glacé cherries, halved, washed and dried
100g (4oz) self-raising flour
75g (3oz) plain flour
25g (1oz) cornflour
175g (6oz) butter, softened
175g (6oz) caster sugar
3 eggs
finely grated rind of 1 lemon
25g (1oz) nibbed almonds

Preparation time: 30 minutes
Cooking time: 1¼ hours
Oven: 180°C, 350°F, Gas Mark 4

1. Grease an 18cm (7 inch) round cake tin and line with greased greaseproof paper.
2. Put the cherries and 25g (1oz) of the self-raising flour in a polythene bag and toss to coat the cherries. Sift the remaining flours and cornflour into a bowl.
3. Cream the butter and sugar together until light and fluffy. Beat in the eggs, one at a time. Stir in the sifted flours, lemon rind, nibbed almonds and cherries.
4. Spoon into the prepared tin and bake in a preheated oven until well risen and golden. Turn out and cool on a wire rack.

Makes an 18cm (7 inch) round cake (8 slices)

Nutrition content per serving   Carbohydrate: 59g   Fat: 22g
Fibre: 1g   Kilocalories: 441

ABOVE: Dark Ginger Cake.
LEFT: Glacé Cherry Cake.

MADEIRA CAKE

225g (8oz) butter, softened
225g (8oz) caster sugar
225g (8oz) self-raising flour
100g (4oz) plain flour
4 eggs
grated rind of 2 lemons
4 teaspoons lemon juice
piece of candied citron peel (optional)

Preparation time: 30 minutes
Cooking time: $1\frac{1}{4}$–$1\frac{1}{2}$ hours
Oven: 160°C, 325°F, Gas Mark 3

1. Line a 20cm (8 inch) round cake tin with greased greaseproof paper.
2. In a mixing bowl, cream the butter and sugar together until light and fluffy. Sift the flours together. Beat the eggs into the creamed mixture following each addition with a spoonful of flour. Fold in the remaining flour, followed by the lemon rind and juice.
3. Turn the mixture into the prepared tin and lay 2 or 3 thin slices of citron peel on top. Bake in a preheated oven for $1\frac{1}{4}$–$1\frac{1}{2}$ hours or until the cake is well risen, firm to the touch and golden brown, and a skewer inserted into the centre comes out clean.
4. Cool in the tin for 10 minutes, then turn on to a wire rack and leave until completely cold.

Makes a 20cm (8 inch) round cake (8 slices)

Nutrition content per serving   Carbohydrate: 61g   Fat: 27g
Fibre: 2g   Kilocalories: 497

EASY APPLE & RAISIN SPONGE

225g (8oz) cooking apples, peeled, cored and
  diced
50g (2oz) caster sugar
75g (3oz) self-raising flour, sifted
$\frac{1}{2}$ teaspoon baking powder
$\frac{1}{4}$ teaspoon salt
25g (1oz) shelled hazelnuts, chopped
50g (2oz) seedless raisins
1 egg, beaten
$\frac{1}{4}$ teaspoon vanilla essence
4 tablespoons cooking oil

Preparation time: 10 minutes
Cooking time: 1–$1\frac{1}{4}$ hours
Oven: 180°C, 350°F, Gas Mark 4

1. Put the apples, sugar, flour, baking powder, salt, nuts and raisins into a bowl.
2. Mix together the egg, vanilla essence and oil and add to the bowl. Stir until well blended.
3. Put into a lightly buttered 900ml ($1\frac{1}{2}$ pint) ovenproof dish. Spread out evenly.
4. Bake in a preheated oven for 1–$1\frac{1}{4}$ hours or until golden brown and slightly shrinking from the sides of the dish. Serve hot with cream or ice cream.

Serves 4–6

Nutrition content per serving   Carbohydrate: 41–27g
Fat: 19–13g   Fibre: 3–2g   Kilocalories: 342–228

COCONUT CHERRY CAKE

350g (12oz) self-raising flour
pinch of salt
175g (6oz) butter
225g (8oz) glacé cherries, quartered
50g (2oz) desiccated coconut
175g (6oz) caster sugar
2 eggs, lightly beaten
generous 150ml ($\frac{1}{4}$ pint) milk

Preparation time: 30 minutes
Cooking time: $1\frac{1}{2}$ hours
Oven: 180°C, 350°F, Gas Mark 4

1. Well grease a 20cm (8 inch) round cake tin and line the bottom with greased greaseproof paper.
2. Sift together the flour and salt. Rub in the butter until the mixture resembles fine breadcrumbs. Toss the cherries in the coconut and add to the mixture with the sugar. Mix lightly. Add the eggs to the mixture with most of the milk. Beat well, then add sufficient extra milk to give a soft dropping consistency.
3. Turn into the prepared tin, level off and bake in a preheated oven for $1\frac{1}{2}$ hours or until well risen and golden brown. Leave in the tin for 5 minutes, then turn out on to a wire rack to cool.

Makes a 20cm (8 inch) round cake (8 slices)

Nutrition content per serving   Carbohydrate: 74g   Fat: 25g
Fibre: 3g   Kilocalories: 525

FROM TOP TO BOTTOM: Madeira Cake; Easy Apple & Raisin Sponge; Coconut Cherry Cake.

firm to the touch, and a skewer comes cut clean. Cool for 15 minutes in the tin, then turn out on to a wire rack to cool completely.
5. Mix the icing sugar with enough milk to make a spreading consistency. Spread quickly and evenly over the cake and leave to dry. Decorate with walnut halves, if liked.

Makes an 18cm (7 inch) ring or square cake (6 slices)

Nutrition content per serving   Carbohydrate: 67g   Fat: 9g
Fibre: 1g   Kilocalories 340

APPLE CRUMB CAKE

TOPPING:
25g (1oz) butter
75g (3oz) self-raising flour
25g (1oz) caster sugar
1 tablespoon water
BASE:
50g (2oz) butter, softened
50g (2oz) caster sugar
1 egg, beaten
few drops of vanilla essence
100g (4oz) self-raising flour
2 cooking apples, peeled, cored and sliced
1 red dessert apple, cored, sliced and lightly
  poached, to finish

Preparation time: 30 minutes
Cooking time: 1 hour
Oven: 180°C, 350°F, Gas Mark 4

1. Grease a 20cm (8 inch) sandwich tin and line the bottom with greased greaseproof paper.
2. For the topping, rub the butter into the flour and stir in the sugar. Sprinkle on the water and mix together until lumpy. Leave on one side.
3. For the base, cream the butter and sugar together until light and fluffy. Beat in the egg and vanilla essence and finally stir in the flour. Spread over the bottom of the prepared tin.
4. Arrange the cooking apple slices on top and cover completely with the crumble topping.
5. Bake in a preheated oven for about 1 hour. Cool slightly before turning out.
6. Decorate with red apple slices and serve with whipped cream.

Makes a 20cm (8 inch) round cake (6 slices)

Nutrition content per serving   Carbohydrate: 42g   Fat: 12g
Fibre: 3g   Kilocalories: 278

MARBLED RING CAKE

50g (2oz) butter, softened
75g (3oz) caster sugar
½ teaspoon vanilla essence
1 egg
100g (4oz) plain flour
½ teaspoon salt
1 teaspoon baking powder
65ml (2½ fl oz) milk
75g (3oz) black treacle
1 teaspoon ground mixed spice
walnut halves, to decorate (optional)
GLACE ICING:
175g (6oz) icing sugar, sifted
about 1 tablespoon milk

Preparation time: 10 minutes
Cooking time: 35–40 minutes
Oven: 180°C, 350°F, Gas Mark 4

1. Grease and flour an 18cm (7 inch) square tin or a tube tin. Cream the butter with the sugar and vanilla. Beat in the egg. Sift the dry ingredients together and stir into the mixture alternately with the milk. Beat for a minute.
2. Spoon about one third of the batter into a small bowl and mix in the treacle and spice.
3. Spoon the light and dark batters alternately into the tin. Run a knife through them in a zigzag pattern, to give the marbled effect.
4. Bake in a preheated oven until the centre is

ABOVE: Marbled Ring Cake.
LEFT: Apple Crumb Cake.

browning too quickly. Leave in the tin for 5 minutes, then turn out to cool on a wire rack and remove the greaseproof paper.
4. Cream the butter and gradually add the icing sugar, lemon rind and juice, beating well to give a spreading consistency. Spread over the top and sides of the cake and swirl up with a knife to give a 'spiked' appearance.

Makes a 23cm (9 inch) round cake (12 slices)

Nutrition content per serving   Carbohydrate: 75g   Fat: 33g
Fibre: 1g   Kilocalories: 599

GOOSEBERRY CAKE

100g (4oz) butter
165g (5½oz) self-raising flour
1 teaspoon baking powder
2 eggs, beaten
100g (4oz) caster sugar
1½ tablespoons white wine
1½ teaspoons orange-flower or rose water
¼ teaspoon grated nutmeg
100g (4oz) gooseberries, topped and tailed
caster sugar, for dredging

Preparation time: 15 minutes
Cooking time: 45 minutes
Oven: 180°C, 350°F, Gas Mark 4

1. Grease an 18–19cm (7–7½ inch) square springform cake tin and line with greased greaseproof paper.
2. Melt the butter in a saucepan and then cool until only just warm.
3. Sift the flour and baking powder and mix into the butter with the eggs, sugar, wine, flavouring and nutmeg; beat well.
4. Pour half the mixture into the prepared tin. Cover with the gooseberries and then add the remaining mixture, making sure the gooseberries are covered.
5. Place in a preheated oven and bake for about 45 minutes or until golden brown and a skewer inserted in the centre comes out clean.
6. Cool in the tin for a few minutes, then remove carefully on to a wire rack. Dredge with sugar and serve hot or cold, with cream if liked.

Makes an 18–19cm (7–7½ inch) square cake (6 slices)

Nutrition content per serving   Carbohydrate: 42g   Fat: 16g
Fibre: 2g   Kilocalories: 323

GLACE PINEAPPLE CAKE

225g (8oz) butter, softened
225g (8oz) caster sugar
4 eggs, beaten
100g (4oz) glacé pineapple, finely chopped
100g (4oz) glacé cherries, washed, dried and
   finely chopped
225g (8oz) plain flour
1 teaspoon baking powder
25g (1oz) shelled walnuts, roughly chopped
50g (2oz) ground almonds
LEMON BUTTERCREAM:
175g (6oz) butter
350g (12oz) icing sugar, sifted
grated rind and juice of 2 lemons

Preparation time: 50 minutes
Cooking time: 1¼–1½ hours
Oven: 180°C, 350°F, Gas Mark 4

1. Grease a 23cm (9 inch) round cake tin and line with greased greaseproof paper.
2. Cream the butter and sugar together until pale and fluffy. Add the eggs, a little at a time, beating well between each addition. Toss the pineapple and cherries in 1 tablespoon of the flour and add to the mixture. Sift the remaining flour and baking powder together and fold into the mixture, together with the nuts.
3. Turn the mixture into the prepared tin and smooth the surface with a knife. Bake in a preheated oven for 1¼–1½ hours or until the cake springs back when lightly touched. Cover the top of the cake with greaseproof paper if it is

ABOVE: Glacé Pineapple Cake.
RIGHT: Gooseberry Cake.

LEMON & ALMOND CAKE

The sharp lemon syrup spooned over the hot upside-down cake gives a distinctive flavour. The cake keeps very well for a week.

25g (1oz) flaked almonds
100g (4oz) butter, softened
100g (4oz) light soft brown sugar
2 eggs, beaten
grated rind of 1 lemon
100g (4oz) wholemeal self-raising flour
SYRUP:
75g (3oz) caster sugar
3–4 tablespoons fresh lemon juice

Preparation time: 20 minutes
Cooking time: 20–25 minutes
Oven: 180°C, 350°F, Gas Mark 4

1. Line the bottom of a 23cm (9 inch) round sandwich tin with non-stick silicone paper or greased greaseproof paper. Thoroughly grease the sides of the tin. Tip the almonds into the tin and shake them around so that they cling to the sides and bottom.
2. Put the butter and sugar into a bowl and cream them together until light and fluffy. Gradually beat in the eggs a tablespoon at a time, then beat in the lemon rind.
3. Fold in the flour until smoothly blended, then spoon the mixture into the prepared tin. Smooth the top.
4. Bake near the centre of a preheated oven for 20–25 minutes until risen and firm to the touch.
5. Meanwhile prepare the syrup. Put the caster sugar into a small basin and stir in the lemon juice. Leave to stand, stirring occasionally.
6. When the cake is cooked remove from the oven and leave in the tin for 1 minute, then turn out upside down on to a wire rack and carefully peel off the lining paper.
7. Spoon the lemon syrup evenly over the hot cake, covering the nuts, allowing it to soak in.

Makes a 23cm (9 inch) round cake (6 slices)

Nutrition content per serving   Carbohydrate: 42g   Fat: 18g
Fibre: 2g   Kilocalories: 341

ROSEWATER CAKE

175g (6oz) plain flour
1 tablespoon baking powder
100g (4oz) butter, softened
50g (2oz) caster sugar
2 tablespoons clear honey
2 eggs, lightly beaten
2 tablespoons rosewater
2 tablespoons milk
75g (3oz) chopped mixed peel
75g (3oz) sultanas
ICING:
200g (7oz) icing sugar
2 tablespoons rosewater
1 tablespoon lemon juice (optional)

Preparation time: 25 minutes
Cooking time: 1 hour 5 minutes
Oven: 180°C, 350°F, Gas Mark 4

1. Grease an 18cm (7 inch) round cake tin and line with greased greaseproof paper. Sift the flour with the baking powder into a large bowl.
2. Whisk the butter, sugar and honey together in a food processor or beat in a large bowl until the mixture is pale and fluffy.
3. Add the eggs, 2 tablespoons at a time, beating well between each addition. If the mixture looks as if it might curdle, fold in 1 tablespoon of flour.
4. Fold in the flour and baking powder, and then add the rosewater and milk, turning the mixture over several times, before adding the mixed peel and sultanas.
5. Pour the mixture into the prepared tin and bake in a preheated oven for 1 hour 5 minutes. Insert a knife into the cake to see if it is cooked: the knife should come out clean. If it is still slightly sticky, give the cake 5 minutes more.
6. Cool the cake for 5 minutes then turn out on to a wire rack, remove the paper and leave to cool completely.
7. Sift the icing sugar into a bowl, add the rosewater and beat until smooth. If the mixture is thick but not pourable, add the lemon juice and beat again.
8. When the cake is cool, put a large plate underneath the wire rack, and pour the icing over the cake, smoothing where necessary with a palette knife dipped in hot water.

Makes an 18cm (7 inch) round cake (8 slices)

Nutrition content per serving   Carbohydrate: 67g   Fat: 12g
Fibre: 1g   Kilocalories: 375

TOP: Lemon & Almond Cake; BOTTOM: Rosewater Cake.

BOOTLEGGERS' CAKE

250ml (8fl oz) milk
1 tablespoon lemon juice
200ml (7fl oz) golden syrup
100g (4oz) caster sugar
2 eggs, lightly beaten
375g (13oz) plain flour
2 teaspoons bicarbonate of soda
1 teaspoon baking powder
1 teaspoon ground cinnamon
1 teaspoon ground ginger
250g (9oz) shredded suet
200g (7oz) shelled walnuts, coarsely chopped
275g (10oz) raisins or sultanas, coarsely chopped
120ml (4fl oz) bourbon, whisky or rum
MOONSHINE GLAZE:
100g (4oz) icing sugar
25g (1oz) butter, softened
2 teaspoons bourbon whisky or rum
1 tablespoon vanilla essence

Preparation time: 15 minutes
Cooking time: 1½ hours
Oven: 160°C, 325°F, Gas Mark 3

1. Grease and flour a deep 23cm (9 inch) round cake tin. Mix the milk and lemon juice and let stand for 5 minutes. Stir together the golden syrup, sugar and eggs.
2. Sift the flour, bicarbonate of soda, baking powder and spices together twice. Tip about one-third of this mixture into a bowl and stir in the suet, nuts and raisins. Sift the remaining flour mixture into the golden syrup mixture, alternating with the milk. Stir in the whisky.
3. Stir in the floured suet, nuts and raisins.
4. Pour the mixture into the prepared tin and bake in a preheated oven until the top of the cake is firm and cracked open (about 1½ hours).
5. Let the cake cool for 10 minutes in the tin on a wire rack, then turn out. While still hot, spoon on the glaze – made by mixing all the ingredients together until smooth. It will drip in glossy runnels down the side. Cool before serving.

Makes a 23cm (9 inch) round cake (12 slices)

Nutrition content per serving   Carbohydrate: 68g   Fat: 29g
Fibre: 4g   Kilocalories: 545

ALMOND LAYER CAKE

4 eggs
100g (4oz) caster sugar
75g (3oz) self-raising flour
50g (2oz) ground almonds
few drops of almond essence
50g (2oz) toasted flaked almonds
triple quantity icing for Iced Walnut Cake (page 8)

Preparation time: 50 minutes
Cooking time: 20 minutes
Oven: 190°C, 375°F, Gas Mark 5

1. Grease a 38 × 30cm (15 × 12 inch) tin and line with greased greaseproof paper.
2. Whisk the eggs and sugar together until thick and the whisk leaves a trail when it is lifted out. Sift in the flour and fold in with the ground almonds and the almond essence.
3. Turn the mixture into the prepared tin and level off. Bake in a preheated oven for 20 minutes or until the cake is pale golden and springs back when lightly pressed. Turn out on to a sheet of greaseproof paper and leave to cool. When cold cut across into three rectangles.
4. Spread some of the icing on two of the rectangles of cake, sprinkle with some of the almonds and sandwich the layers together. Spread the remaining icing all over the cake and sprinkle with the remaining almonds. Leave to set in a cool place before serving.

Makes a 30 × 13cm (12 × 5 inch) sandwich cake (8 slices)

Nutrition content per serving   Carbohydrate: 87g   Fat: 10g
Fibre: 2g   Kilocalories: 442

ABOVE: Bootleggers' Cake.
RIGHT: Almond Layer Cake.

MOIST APPLE-SPICE CAKE

275g (10oz) self-raising flour
1 teaspoon salt
½ teaspoon ground cinnamon
¼ teaspoon ground cloves
100g (4oz) butter, softened
225g (8oz) caster sugar
1 egg, lightly beaten
1 teaspoon vanilla essence
350g (12oz) cooking apples, peeled, cored and
    grated
1 teaspoon clear honey
1 tablespoon toasted flaked almonds

Preparation time: 40 minutes
Cooking time: 1¼ hours
Oven: 180°C, 350°F, Gas Mark 4

1. Grease an 18cm (7 inch) square cake tin and
line with greased greaseproof paper.
2. Sift the flour with the salt and spices twice.
Cream the butter and sugar together until pale
and fluffy. Gradually beat in the egg and vanilla
essence. Stir in the apple and fold in the flour.
3. Turn the mixture into the prepared tin and
smooth the top. Bake in a preheated oven for
1¼ hours or until lightly browned and the sides
are shrinking from the tin. Leave in the tin for 5
minutes, then turn on to a wire rack to cool.
4. Remove the greaseproof paper. Brush the top
with honey and sprinkle with the nuts.

Makes an 18cm (7 inch) square cake (6 slices)

Nutrition content per serving   Carbohydrate: 81g   Fat: 17g
Fibre: 3g   Kilocalories: 475

CHOCOLATE POUND CAKE

225g (8oz) granulated sugar
65ml (2½ fl oz) water
65g (2½oz) cocoa powder
225g (8oz) unsalted butter, softened
225g (8oz) caster sugar
5 eggs, separated
225g (8oz) plain flour, sifted
¼ teaspoon bicarbonate of soda
pinch of salt
icing sugar, to finish

Preparation time: 35 minutes
Cooking time: about 1½ hours
Oven: 160°C, 325°F, Gas Mark 3

1. Dissolve the granulated sugar in the water in
a heavy saucepan, stirring constantly. Bring to
the boil and cook to 102°C (215°F) on a sugar
thermometer. Remove the pan from the heat
and dip its base in cold water to arrest further
cooking. Add the cocoa powder and stir until
smooth. Leave to cool.
2. Butter a 23 × 13cm (9 × 5 inch) loaf tin and
line with greased greaseproof paper. Brush the
paper with melted butter and dust with flour.
3. Cream the butter with the caster sugar until
light and fluffy. Add the egg yolks, 1 at a time,
beating well. Stir in the chocolate syrup.
4. Sift the flour, bicarbonate of soda and salt
together into the bowl and fold into the
chocolate mixture. Whisk the egg whites until
stiff. Gently fold a third of the egg whites into
the mixture, then fold in the rest.
5. Pour the mixture into the tin and bake in a
preheated oven for 1¼ hours or until a skewer
inserted into the centre comes out clean.
Remove to a wire rack and leave the cake in the
tin for 10 minutes before turning it out to cool
completely. When cool, remove the lining
paper. Dust with icing sugar before serving.

Makes a 23 × 13cm (9 × 5 inch) loaf cake (12 slices)

Nutrition content per serving   Carbohydrate: 55g   Fat: 19g
Fibre: 1g   Kilocalories: 402

ABOVE: Moist Apple-Spice Cake.
LEFT: Chocolate Pound Cake.

Fruit cakes
◆
& TEABREADS

Teatime is a great British institution, with its delicious cakes and breads. Traditionally, the cakes served with tea are not too sweet, and they usually contain spices plus a lot of fruit and nuts. The recipes in this chapter include an economical fruit cake that can be covered with marzipan and royal icing to be used as a Christmas cake, and a richly fruited cake made without flour. Another fruit cake is flavoured with scented Earl Grey tea. The teabreads here contain many fruits – prunes, dates, apples, cranberries, bananas – and nuts such as walnuts, hazelnuts and peanuts. There is even a delicious cake made with grated carrots.

Light Fruit Cake (see recipe on page 26).

LIGHT FRUIT CAKE

50g (2oz) glacé cherries, roughly chopped
175g (6oz) currants
175g (6oz) sultanas
50g (2oz) ground almonds
100g (4oz) chopped mixed peel
225g (8oz) butter, softened
225g (8oz) caster or soft light brown sugar
4 eggs, beaten
225g (8oz) plain flour
1 teaspoon ground mixed spice
½ teaspoon ground cinnamon
grated rind of 1 orange
2 tablespoons orange juice
2 tablespoons milk

Preparation time: 30 minutes
Cooking time: about 2½ hours
Oven: 160°C, 325°F, Gas Mark 3

1. Grease a 20cm (8 inch) round cake tin and line with greased greaseproof paper. Mix the fruit, almonds and peel in a bowl.
2. In a separate bowl cream the butter and sugar together until very light, fluffy and pale. Beat in the eggs one at a time.
3. Sift the flour with the spices and fold into the mixture with the orange rind, followed by the orange juice and milk. Add the fruit mixture.
4. Turn into the prepared tin and bake in a preheated oven for about 2½ hours or until a skewer inserted in the centre comes out clean.
5. Leave to cool completely in the tin.

Makes a 20cm (8 inch) round cake (12 slices)

Nutrition content per serving   Carbohydrate: 61g   Fat: 20g
Fibre: 3g   Kilocalories: 429

EARL GREY FRUIT CAKE

50g (2oz) sultanas
50g (2oz) raisins
50g (2oz) currants
1 teaspoon grated lemon rind
100g (4oz) demerara sugar
150ml (¼ pint) cold strong Earl Grey tea
1 egg, beaten
225g (8oz) self-raising flour

Preparation time: 10 minutes, plus soaking
Cooking time: 1 hour
Oven: 160°C, 325°F, Gas Mark 3

1. Place the sultanas, raisins and currants in a bowl. Add the lemon rind and all but 1 teaspoon of the demerara sugar. Pour the strained tea over the top, mix well, then cover and leave to soak overnight.
2. Grease a 20 × 10cm (8 × 4 inch) loaf tin and line with greased greaseproof paper.
3. Add the beaten egg to the dried fruit mixture and combine well. Sift the flour into the mixture and fold in gently with a metal spoon.
4. Place the mixture in the prepared tin. Sprinkle with the reserved demerara sugar.
5. Place in a preheated oven and bake for about 1 hour. Turn out on to a wire rack to cool.

Makes a 20 × 10cm (8 × 4 inch) loaf cake (8 slices)

Nutrition content per serving   Carbohydrate: 47g   Fat: 1g
Fibre: 2g   Kilocalories: 200

HAZELNUT & CARROT CAKE

225g (8oz) carrots
3 eggs, separated
150g (5oz) caster sugar
150g (5oz) shelled hazelnuts, finely chopped
2 teaspoons finely grated lemon rind
50g (2oz) plain flour
½ teaspoon baking powder
icing sugar, to finish

Preparation time: 40 minutes
Cooking time: 40–45 minutes
Oven: 180°C, 350°F, Gas Mark 4

1. Well grease an 18cm (7 inch) square tin.
2. Peel and grate the carrots and re-weigh; you should have about 150g (5oz). Whisk the egg yolks and the sugar until thick and creamy. Stir in the carrots, hazelnuts and lemon rind. Sift in the flour and baking powder and fold in. Whisk the egg whites until stiff, then fold in.
3. Turn into the tin and bake in a preheated oven for 40–45 minutes. Leave in the tin for 2–3 minutes, then turn out on to a wire rack to cool. Dredge with icing sugar before serving.

Makes an 18cm (7 inch) square cake (8 slices)

Nutrition content per serving   Carbohydrate: 28g   Fat: 9g
Fibre: 2g   Kilocalories: 203

TOP: Earl Grey Fruit Cake; BOTTOM: Hazelnut & Carrot Cake.

WALNUT STREUSEL LOAF

100g (4oz) demerara sugar
25g (1oz) butter, melted
100g (4oz) shelled walnuts, chopped
1 teaspoon ground cinnamon
CAKE:
100g (4oz) black treacle
150ml ($\frac{1}{4}$ pint) milk
2 eggs, beaten
275g (10oz) self-raising flour
50g (2oz) butter
100g (4oz) stoned dates, chopped

Preparation time: 40 minutes
Cooking time: 1 hour
Oven: 180°C, 350°F, Gas Mark 4

1. Grease a 23 × 13cm (9 × 5 inch) loaf tin.
2. Mix together the sugar, butter, walnuts and cinnamon.
3. Blend together the treacle, milk and beaten eggs. Sift the flour into a bowl and rub in the butter. Add the dates and treacle mixture.
4. Turn half the cake mixture into the prepared tin and sprinkle with half the streusel mixture. Cover with the remaining cake mixture and top with the last of the streusel mixture.
5. Bake in a preheated oven for 1 hour. Leave in the tin for 5 minutes, then cool on a wire rack.

Makes a 23 × 13cm (9 × 5 inch) loaf cake (12 slices)

Nutrition content per serving   Carbohydrate: 39g   Fat: 11g
Fibre: 2g   Kilocalories: 265

PEANUT & CRANBERRY CAKE

150g (6oz) self-raising flour
$\frac{3}{4}$ teaspoon baking powder
100g (4oz) wholewheat flour
100g (4oz) butter
100g (4oz) light soft brown sugar
grated rind of 1 lemon
100g (4oz) cranberries, roughly chopped
75g (3oz) peanuts, shelled and roughly chopped
50g (2oz) chopped mixed peel
2 eggs, beaten with 4 tablespoons milk

Preparation time: 20 minutes
Cooking time: 1 hour 10 minutes
Oven: 180°C, 350°F, Gas Mark 4

1. Grease a 23 × 13cm (9 × 5 inch) loaf tin and line with greased greaseproof paper.
2. Sift the self-raising flour and baking powder into a bowl and mix in the wholewheat flour. Rub in the butter.
3. Stir in the sugar, lemon rind, cranberries, peanuts and peel. Add the eggs and milk.
4. Turn into the tin and roughly level the top. Place in a preheated oven and bake for about 1 hour 10 minutes or until cooked.
5. Turn out on to a wire rack and leave to cool. Wrap in foil and keep for 24 hours before cutting.

Makes a 23 × 13cm (9 × 5 inch) loaf cake (12 slices)

Nutrition content per serving   Carbohydrate: 19g   Fat: 10g
Fibre: 2g   Kilocalories: 214

SPICY TEABREAD

450g (1 lb) self-raising flour
1 teaspoon salt
1 teaspoon ground mixed spice
$\frac{1}{2}$ teaspoon ground cinnamon
175g (6oz) soft brown sugar
100g (4oz) butter
2 eggs, beaten
2 tablespoons black treacle
scant 300ml ($\frac{1}{2}$ pint) milk
$\frac{1}{2}$ egg, beaten, to glaze

Preparation time: 30 minutes
Cooking time: 45 minutes – 1 hour
Oven: 190°C, 375°F, Gas Mark 5

1. Grease a 23 × 13cm (9 × 5 inch) loaf tin.
2. Sift the flour, salt, spice and cinnamon into a mixing bowl. Stir in the sugar. Rub in the butter. Mix the eggs, treacle and half of the milk together and stir into the flour mixture. Gradually stir in the remaining milk until the mixture drops easily from the spoon.
3. Spoon the mixture into the prepared tin. Bake in a preheated oven for 45 minutes to 1 hour or until a skewer inserted in the centre comes out clean. Brush with the beaten egg after 30 minutes. Cool on a wire rack.

Makes a 23 × 13cm (9 × 5 inch) loaf cake (12 slices)

Nutrition content per serving   Carbohydrate: 47g   Fat: 9g
Fibre: 1g   Kilocalories: 285

FROM TOP TO BOTTOM: Walnut Streusel Loaf; Peanut & Cranberry Cake; Spicy Teabread.

BANANA HONEY TEABREAD

225g (8oz) butter, softened
225g (8oz) caster sugar
2 tablespoons thick honey
4 eggs, beaten
450g (1 lb) self-raising flour
½ teaspoon salt
½ teaspoon bicarbonate of soda
4 medium ripe bananas, peeled and mashed
100g (4oz) shelled walnuts, roughly chopped

Preparation time: 25 minutes
Cooking time: about 1¼ hours
Oven: 180°C, 350°F, Gas Mark 4

1. Grease two 23 × 13cm (9 × 5 inch) loaf tins and line with greased greaseproof paper.
2. Put the butter, sugar and honey in a bowl and beat together until light and fluffy. Beat in the eggs a little at a time, adding a little flour with each addition. Sift the remaining flour, salt and soda together, then fold into the creamed mixture. Beat in the bananas and nuts.
3. Spoon the mixture into the prepared tins. Bake just below the centre of a preheated oven for 1¼ hours or until well risen and a skewer inserted in the centre comes out clean.
4. Leave to cool in the tins, then remove the greaseproof paper. Wrap each cake in foil, overwrap in polythene bags and store in airtight containers. Serve cut into thick slices, spread with butter if liked.

Makes two 23 × 13cm (9 × 5 inch) loaf cakes (12 slices each)

Nutrition content per serving   Carbohydrate: 56g   Fat: 22g
Fibre: 3g   Kilocalories: 435

EASY NO-FLOUR FRUIT CAKE

450g (1 lb) mincemeat
450g (1 lb) mixed dried fruit
100g (4oz) glacé cherries, halved
100g (4oz) shelled walnuts, chopped
225g (8oz) cornflakes, crushed
3 eggs, lightly beaten
1 large can condensed milk, equivalent to
   1.12 litres (1⅞ pints) skimmed milk
1 teaspoon ground mixed spice
1 teaspoon baking powder

Preparation time: 25 minutes
Cooking time: 1¼ hours
Oven: 150°C, 300°F, Gas Mark 2

1. Grease a 25cm (10 inch) round cake tin and line the bottom with greased greaseproof paper.
2. Put all the ingredients into a mixing bowl and blend well. Turn into the prepared cake tin and level off.
3. Bake in a preheated oven for 1¼ hours. Leave in the tin for 10 minutes, then turn out on to a wire rack to cool.

Makes a 25cm (10 inch) round cake (12 slices)

Nutrition content per serving   Carbohydrate: 87g   Fat: 8g
Fibre: 6g   Kilocalories: 414

PRUNE & NUT TEABREAD

225g (8oz) wholewheat self-raising flour
pinch of salt
pinch of grated nutmeg
¼ teaspoon ground allspice
1 teaspoon grated orange rind
25g (1oz) butter, softened
75g (3oz) shelled walnuts, chopped
75g (3oz) prunes, stoned and chopped
1 egg
100ml (3½ fl oz) buttermilk or skimmed milk
3 tablespoons orange juice

Preparation time: 15 minutes
Cooking time: 45 minutes
Oven: 190°C, 375°F, Gas Mark 5

1. Grease a 15cm (6 inch) round cake tin.
2. Sift the flour, salt, nutmeg and allspice into a mixing bowl, tip in any bran remaining in the sieve and stir in the orange rind. Rub in the butter, using a fork. Stir in the walnuts and prunes. Beat the egg with the buttermilk or milk and the orange juice. Pour on to the dry ingredients and mix quickly to a stiff batter.
3. Turn the mixture into the prepared tin. Bake in a preheated oven for 40–45 minutes or until the teabread is well risen and golden brown and a fine skewer pierced through the centre comes out clean. Stand the tin on a wire rack to cool, then turn out the teabread and allow to become cold. Serve spread with soft cheese and honey.

Makes a 15cm (6 inch) round cake (8 slices)

Nutrition content per serving   Carbohydrate: 24g   Fat: 9g
Fibre: 5g   Kilocalories: 193

FROM TOP TO BOTTOM: Banana Honey Teabread; Easy No-Flour Fruit Cake; Prune & Nut Teabread.

DATE & WALNUT CAKE

300ml (½ pint) boiling water
225g (8oz) stoned dates, chopped
1 teaspoon bicarbonate of soda
225g (8oz) caster sugar
75g (3oz) butter, softened
1 egg, beaten
275g (10oz) plain flour
1 teaspoon baking powder
½ teaspoon salt
50g (2oz) shelled walnuts, chopped
walnut halves, to decorate
TOPPING:
65g (2½oz) brown sugar
25g (1oz) butter
2 tablespoons milk

Preparation time: 30 minutes
Cooking time: 1 hour
Oven: 180°C, 350°F, Gas Mark 4

1. Grease a 23cm (9 inch) square tin and line it with greased greaseproof paper.
2. Put the water, dates and bicarbonate of soda in a bowl and leave to stand for 5 minutes. Cream the sugar and butter together until fluffy, then stir in the egg with the water and dates. Sift the flour with the baking powder and salt and fold in with the walnuts. Turn into the tin and smooth the top.
3. Bake in a preheated oven for 1 hour. Turn out and leave to cool on a wire rack.
4. Place all the topping ingredients in a pan and boil for 3 minutes, then spread over the cake. Decorate with walnut halves, and leave to set.

Makes a 23cm (9 inch) square cake (8 slices)

Nutrition content per serving   Carbohydrate: 84g   Fat: 15g
Fibre: 4g   Kilocalories: 471

APPLE, DATE & SESAME LOAF

350g (12oz) self-raising wheatmeal flour
¼ teaspoon salt
¼ teaspoon grated nutmeg
¼ teaspoon ground allspice
¼ teaspoon ground mace
¼ teaspoon ground cardamom
¼ teaspoon ground ginger
1 teaspoon ground cinnamon
grated rind of ½ lemon
50g (2oz) Barbados or molasses sugar
2 eggs (size 1 or 2), beaten
150ml (¼ pint) plain unsweetened yogurt
1 large cooking apple, peeled, cored and grated
225g (8oz) stoned dates, chopped
50g (2oz) sesame seeds

Preparation time: 15–20 minutes plus storing
Cooking time: 1½–1¾ hours
Oven: 160°C, 325°F, Gas Mark 3

1. Grease and lightly flour a 23 × 13cm (9 × 5 inch) loaf tin.
2. Sift the flour, salt and spices into a large mixing bowl, tipping in any bran left in the sieve. Stir in the lemon rind and sugar and make a well in the centre. Pour in the eggs and yogurt and gradually mix the dry ingredients into the liquid. Stir in the apple, dates and 25g (1oz) of the sesame seeds.
3. Shape the mixture into a loaf and put into the prepared tin. Press down the corners and smooth the top with the back of a spoon. Scatter over the rest of the sesame seeds and press them into the top of the loaf.
4. Bake in the centre of a preheated oven for 1½–1¾ hours until well risen and lightly browned. Allow the loaf to cool in the tin for 5–10 minutes before turning it out on to a wire rack to cool completely. Store for at least 1 day before serving, sliced and buttered.

Makes a 23 × 13cm (9 × 5 inch) loaf cake (12 slices)

Nutrition content per serving   Carbohydrate: 39g   Fat: 4g
Fibre: 5g   Kilocalories: 209

TOP: Apple, Date & Sesame Loaf; BOTTOM: Date & Walnut Cake.

Dessert cakes
& GÂTEAUX

A beautifully decorated cake makes a magnificent and impressive dinner party dessert. Whipped cream, ice-cream, luscious fruits and spirits are what make these cakes special.

The cakes in this chapter range from rich creamed mixtures and whisked sponges to a choux pastry ring, crumbly scone-type layers, nut meringue discs, a sweet buttery yeast cake soaked in a sugar syrup, and heavenly baked cheesecakes. There is also a recipe for a rich and sticky Italian Christmas cake, containing candied fruits and peel, nuts and honey, and a frozen cake made simply from whipped cream, egg whites and hazelnuts and flavoured with Amaretto liqueur.

Pear & Ginger Gâteau (see recipe on page 36).

PEAR & GINGER GATEAU

3 eggs
90g (3½oz) caster sugar
75g (3oz) plain flour, sifted
1 × 400g (14oz) can pear quarters, drained
50g (2oz) crystallized ginger, a few pieces
    reserved for decoration, the rest chopped
600ml (1 pint) double or whipping cream,
    whipped to form stiff peaks
small cone-shaped brandy snaps

Preparation time: 40–45 minutes
Cooking time: 30–40 minutes
Oven: 180°C, 350°F, Gas Mark 4

1. Grease the inside of a 19cm (7½ inch) moule à manqué or cake tin with butter and dust the sides with flour. Place a circle of greaseproof paper in the bottom.
2. Place the eggs and sugar in a large bowl and whisk over a pan of hot water until the mixture is thick and creamy. Remove from the heat and beat until cool. (No heat is needed if using an electric mixer.)
3. Fold the flour in carefully in three batches. Pour into the prepared tin and bake in a preheated oven for about 30 minutes, until the sponge is golden brown, springy to the touch and starts to leave the sides of the tin. Turn out the cake on to a wire rack and leave until cold. When the sponge is cold, slice it into two layers.
4. Reserve 8 pear quarters and chop the rest. Mix them with the chopped ginger and 3–4 tablespoons of the cream.
5. Sandwich the sponge with the ginger cream mixture.
6. Coat the outside of the sponge with most of the cream.
7. Pipe cream into the centre of the brandy snap cones. Arrange them alternately with the reserved pear quarters on top of the sponge.
8. Crush enough brandy snaps to coat the sides of the gâteau. Press on the pieces with a broad-bladed knife.
9. Pipe around the top edge of the sponge with small rosettes of cream and decorate with the reserved pieces of crystallized ginger. Place on a plate and refrigerate until required.

Serves 6

Nutrition content per serving   Carbohydrate: 50g   Fat: 53g
Fibre: 1g   Kilocalories: 691

RASPBERRY ICE-CREAM CAKE

3 eggs, separated
4 tablespoons hot water
175g (6oz) caster sugar
¼ teaspoon vanilla essence
2 teaspoons finely grated lemon rind
175g (6oz) plain flour
50g (2oz) cornflour
1 tablespoon baking powder
FILLING:
1 litre (2 pints) dairy ice-cream
225g (8oz) fresh raspberries
TO DECORATE:
icing sugar, sifted
fresh raspberries
fresh mint sprigs

Preparation time: 40 minutes
Cooking time: 25 minutes
Oven: 200°C, 400°F, Gas Mark 6

1. Well grease a 23cm (9 inch) cake tin and line the bottom with greased greaseproof paper.
2. Whisk the egg yolks with the water, sugar, vanilla essence and lemon rind until the mixture is thick and creamy. Sift together the flour, cornflour and baking powder. Whisk the egg whites until they stand in stiff peaks. Fold the flours into the egg yolk mixture, then the egg whites.
3. Turn into the prepared tin and bake in a preheated oven for 25 minutes or until well risen and golden brown. Leave in the tin for 5 minutes, then turn out and cool on a wire rack.
4. Just before serving split the cake into two layers. Put spoonfuls of ice-cream on the bottom layer and top with the raspberries. Replace the top layer of the cake and sprinkle with icing sugar. Decorate with raspberries and mint sprigs. Serve as soon as possible.

Serves 6–8

Nutrition content per serving   Carbohydrate: 88–66g   Fat: 9–7g
Fibre: 4–3g   Kilocalories: 448–336

Raspberry Ice-Cream Cake.

STRAWBERRY GATEAU

3 eggs
75g (3oz) caster sugar
75g (3oz) plain flour, sifted
350g (12oz) strawberries, washed and hulled
300ml (½ pint) double cream, whipped until stiff
2 tablespoons Amaretto liqueur
175g (6oz) redcurrant jelly
1 tablespoon water
175g (6oz) marzipan

Preparation time: 40 minutes
Cooking time: 20 minutes
Oven: 200°C, 400°F, Gas Mark 6

1. Grease three 20cm (8 inch) sandwich tins and line the bottoms with greased greaseproof paper. Flour the tins, shaking out excess flour.
2. Whisk the eggs and sugar together over hot water for about 5 minutes, until pale and thick. Remove from the heat and continue whisking for a further 5 minutes. (No heat is needed if using an electric mixer.)
3. Fold in the flour with a metal spoon, then turn into the prepared tins. Bake in a preheated oven for 10 minutes, until risen and firm to the touch. Cool on a wire rack.
4. Halve sufficient strawberries to cover one layer of sponge completely. Mash the remaining fruit with a fork.
5. Put half the cream into a piping bag fitted with a star nozzle. Fold the crushed strawberries into the remaining cream.
6. Sprinkle the two plain layers of sponge with Amaretto and sandwich together with half the strawberry cream. Top with the remaining strawberry cream and then place the third sponge layer covered with strawberries on top.
7. Melt the redcurrant jelly with the water.
8. Using a piece of string, measure the circumference and height of the cake. Roll out the marzipan to the exact size. Brush with redcurrant jelly and carefully press on to the sides of the cake. Use the remaining redcurrant jelly to glaze the top of the cake. Chill.
9. Pipe a decorative border of cream around the edge of the cake before serving.

Serves 8

Nutrition content per serving   Carbohydrate: 48g   Fat: 26g
Fibre: 3g   Kilocalories: 442

ABOVE: Strawberry Gâteau.
LEFT: Lemon Cream Sponge.

LEMON CREAM SPONGE

3 eggs
75g (3oz) caster sugar
75g (3oz) self-raising flour
150ml (¼ pint) double cream, whipped
2 tablespoons lemon curd
TO DECORATE:
sifted icing sugar
sugared shreds of lemon rind
twisted lemon slices

Preparation time: 30 minutes
Cooking time: 20 minutes
Oven: 190°C, 375°F, Gas Mark 5

1. Grease two 18cm (7 inch) sandwich tins and line them with greased greaseproof paper.
2. Put the eggs and sugar in a heatproof bowl over a pan of hot water and whisk until the mixture is thick and creamy. Remove from the heat and whisk for a further 2 minutes. (If using an electric mixer, no heat is needed.) Sift in the flour and carefully fold it in.
3. Divide the mixture between the tins and bake in a preheated oven for 20 minutes, or until the tops spring back when lightly pressed with the fingertips. Turn on to a wire rack to cool.
4. Mix the cream with the lemon curd and use to sandwich the cooled cakes. Dredge the top with icing sugar, decorate and serve.

Serves 6

Nutrition content per serving   Carbohydrate: 28g   Fat: 15g
Fibre: 0g   Kilocalories: 264

CARIBBEAN COFFEE GATEAU

6 eggs
1 tablespoon coffee essence
175g (6oz) caster sugar
150g (5oz) plain flour
25g (1oz) cornflour
4 tablespoons rum
50g (2oz) plain chocolate, grated
COFFEE BUTTERCREAM:
175g (6oz) butter
350g (12oz) icing sugar, sifted
1–1½ tablespoons coffee essence

Preparation time: 45 minutes
Cooking time: 25 minutes
Oven: 190°C, 375°F, Gas Mark 5

1. Grease two 23cm (9 inch) sandwich tins and line the bottoms with greased greaseproof paper.
2. In a bowl over a pan of simmering water, whisk the eggs, coffee essence and caster sugar together until very thick and creamy. Remove from the heat. (If using an electric mixer no heat is needed.) Gently fold in the sifted flours.
3. Divide the mixture equally between the two tins and bake in a preheated oven for 25 minutes or until the cake springs back when lightly pressed. Leave in the tins for 5 minutes, then turn out and cool on a wire rack.
4. To make the buttercream, beat the butter until soft, then gradually beat in the sugar alternately with the coffee essence. Continue beating until light and fluffy.
5. Sprinkle the rum over the surface of the cakes. Sandwich the cakes together with some of the buttercream and use the rest to cover the top of the cake. Sprinkle over the grated chocolate.

Serves 8–10

Nutrition content per serving   Carbohydrate: 93–75g
Fat: 24–20g   Fibre: 1g   Kilocalories: 616–493

AMERICAN STRAWBERRY SHORTCAKE

225g (8oz) plain flour
1 tablespoon baking powder
½ teaspoon salt
50g (2oz) caster sugar
50g (2oz) butter
about 150ml (¼ pint) milk
350g (12oz) ripe strawberries, or 275g (10oz) frozen berries
150ml (¼ pint) whipping cream, whipped with 1 teaspoon caster sugar (optional)

Preparation time: about 15 minutes
Cooking time: about 10 minutes
Oven: 220°C, 425°F, Gas Mark 7

1. Sift the flour, baking powder and salt together and stir in the sugar. Cut in the butter with a pastry scraper or round-bladed knife.
2. Stir in just enough milk to make a soft dough. On a lightly floured board, pat – do not roll – the dough out to a 30cm (12 inch) wide oblong. Cut out two 15cm (6 inch) rounds.
3. Lay the pastry rounds on a lightly greased baking sheet and bake in a preheated oven for about 10 minutes, until risen and brown.
4. Reserve 10–12 of the best berries. Lightly crush or halve the remainder and spread on one shortcake layer. Spread on some of the cream. Add the second layer and 'frost' with the remaining cream. Decorate with the reserved berries.

Serves 4–6

Nutrition content per serving   Carbohydrate: 68–45g
Fat: 25–17g   Fibre: 4–3g   Kilocalories: 517–345

ABOVE: Caribbean Coffee Gâteau.
RIGHT: American Strawberry Shortcake.

LINDY'S CHEESECAKE

shortcrust pastry made with 120g (4½oz) plain
*   flour, sifted, 120g (4½oz) butter, chilled and*
*   diced, 40g (1½oz) caster sugar, 1 teaspoon*
*   grated lemon rind, 1 egg yolk*
candied orange peel, to decorate
icing sugar, to finish
FILLING:
1 kg (2 lb) curd cheese
350g (12oz) caster sugar
40g (1½oz) plain flour
2 tablespoons grated orange rind
1 tablespoon grated lemon rind
2 egg yolks
5 eggs
100ml (3½ fl oz) double cream

Preparation time: 45 minutes plus cooling
Cooking time: 1¾ hours
Oven: 200°C, 400°F, Gas Mark 6; then 230°C,
450°F, Gas Mark 8; then 110°C, 225°F,
Gas Mark ¼

1. Remove the sides of a 24cm (9½ inch)
springform tin and grease the base. Roll out half
the pastry and line the base. Prick all over and
par-bake in a preheated oven for 15 minutes.
Cool. Increase the oven temperature.
2. Roll out the remaining pastry to the same
thickness as the base and cut out two strips the
depth of the tin, to line the sides.
3. Grease the sides of the tin and snap back on
to the base. Line with the pastry strips, pressing
them lightly but firmly into the pastry base.
4. Beat the curd cheese with the sugar and
flour. Beat in the rinds and the egg yolks, one at
a time. Beat in the eggs, then the cream.
5. Pour the filling into the case and bake in a
preheated oven for 15 minutes, then reduce the
oven temperature and bake for a further 1¼
hours (test with a fine skewer after 1 hour). Cool
in the tin on a wire rack.
6. To serve, carefully remove the sides of the
tin and set the cake on a serving plate. Decorate
with candied peel and finish with icing sugar.
Serve with an orange sauce, if liked.

Serves 10–12

Nutrition content per serving   Carbohydrate: 55–46g
Fat: 24–20g   Fibre: 1g   Kilocalories: 498–415

FROM TOP TO BOTTOM: Austrian Baked Cheesecake;
Lindy's Cheesecake; Biscuit Tortoni.

AUSTRIAN BAKED CHEESECAKE

100g (4oz) butter
100g (4oz) caster sugar
4 eggs, separated
1 teaspoon grated lemon rind
100g (4oz) curd cheese
100g (4oz) ground almonds
icing sugar, to decorate

Preparation time: 30 minutes
Cooking time: 45 minutes
Oven: 180°C, 350°F, Gas Mark 4

1. Grease and flour a 24cm (9½ inch)
springform tin.
2. Beat the butter until light and fluffy. Beat in
the sugar and egg yolks, one at a time. Mix in
the lemon rind, curd cheese and ground
almonds.
3. Whisk the egg whites until stiff and fold into
the cheese mixture.
4. Pour the mixture into the tin. Bake in a
preheated oven for 45 minutes until well risen
and golden. Cool in the tin on a wire rack.
5. Remove sides of tin and set the cheesecake on
a plate. Place strips of paper on top and sprinkle
icing sugar over. Remove the paper.

Serves 6

Nutrition content per serving   Carbohydrate: 21g   Fat: 27g
Fibre: 2g   Kilocalories: 362

BISCUIT TORTONI

2 egg whites
4 tablespoons caster sugar
300ml (½ pint) whipping cream, whipped
175g (6oz) toasted almonds, chopped
4 tablespoons Amaretto liqueur

Preparation time: 20 minutes, plus freezing

1. Whisk the egg whites until stiff. Gradually
whisk in the sugar until thick and glossy.
2. Fold in the cream with half the almonds and
the Amaretto liqueur. Spoon into a 1.2 litre (2
pint) loaf tin, cover and freeze.
3. Unmould on to a plate. Press the remaining
almonds all over the loaf. Freeze until required.

Serves 6–8

Nutrition content per serving   Carbohydrate: 16–12g
Fat: 40–30g   Fibre: 4–3g   Kilocalories: 463–347

a little hot milk. Add to the rest of the milk in the pan and cook gently, stirring, until thick. Mix in the vanilla and butter, then cool.
6. Fold the cream through the custard, then fold in the strawberries and any liqueur.
7. Cut off the top third of the choux ring. Stand the base on a serving dish. Fill with the strawberry cream and replace the lid.
8. Dredge the top with icing sugar and put the unhulled strawberries in the centre. Serve within 2 hours of assembling.

Serves 10–12

Nutrition content per serving   Carbohydrate: 24–20g
Fat: 25–21g   Fibre: 1g   Kilocalories: 347–289

PARIS-BREST

CHOUX PASTE:
75g (3oz) butter
225ml (7½ fl oz) water
95g (3¾oz) plain flour
3 eggs, beaten with a pinch of salt
FILLING:
450g (1 lb) strawberries, all but a few hulled
3 tablespoons orange liqueur or brandy
300ml (½ pint) milk
50g (2 oz) caster sugar
20g (¾oz) plain flour
15g (½oz) cornflour
1 egg
1 egg yolk
few drops of vanilla essence
knob of butter
300ml (½ pint) double cream, whipped
icing sugar, to finish

Preparation time: 1 hour, plus macerating
Cooking time: 45–50 minutes
Oven: 200°C, 400°F, Gas Mark 6

1. To make the choux paste, melt the butter in the water and bring to the boil. Remove from the heat, tip in the flour and beat to a smooth paste. Gradually beat in the eggs to make a glossy paste of piping consistency.
2. Grease a baking sheet and stand a greased 25cm (10 inch) flan ring on it. Spread the paste in a 5cm (2 inch) edging inside the ring.
3. Bake in a preheated oven for 40 minutes or until well risen, golden brown and firm to the touch. Make a few holes in the sides to allow steam to escape and leave to cool on a wire rack.
4. Slice the hulled strawberries. Put in a bowl with the liqueur and macerate for 2 hours.
5. Heat the milk in a heavy saucepan. Beat the sugar, flours, egg and yolk together, then stir in

PANFORTE

75g (3oz) blanched hazelnuts, toasted and chopped
75g (3oz) blanched almonds, toasted and chopped
250g (9oz) candied fruit and peel, chopped
2 teaspoons ground cinnamon
large pinch of ground mixed spice
75g (3oz) plain flour, sifted
100g (4oz) thick honey
90g (3½oz) caster sugar
icing sugar, for dredging

Preparation time: 25 minutes
Cooking time: about 55 minutes
Oven: 150°C, 300°F, Gas Mark 2

1. Using rice paper, line an 18–20cm (7–8 inch) plain flan ring standing on a baking sheet.
2. Combine the nuts, peel and fruits. Sift in the spices and flour and stir until evenly mixed.
3. Put the honey and sugar into a saucepan and bring slowly to the boil. Pour on to the nut mixture and stir well until evenly blended.
4. Place in the tin, levelling the top but not pressing down too firmly. Bake in a preheated oven for 50 minutes or until almost firm.
5. Cool in the tin and then remove carefully.
6. Dredge the top heavily with sifted icing sugar and store wrapped in foil.

Serves 10–12

Nutrition content per serving   Carbohydrate: 36–30g   Fat: 7–6g
Fibre: 2–1g   Kilocalories: 209–174

ABOVE: Paris-Brest.
RIGHT: Panforte.

CHESTNUT VACHERIN

4 egg whites
225g (8oz) caster sugar
½ teaspoon vanilla essence
100g (4oz) shelled hazelnuts, finely ground
FILLING:
225g (8oz) canned chestnut purée
50g (2oz) icing sugar, sifted
2 tablespoons rum
150ml (¼ pint) double or whipping cream
TO FINISH:
150ml (¼ pint) double or whipping cream
25g (1oz) plain chocolate, coarsely grated
25–50g (1–2oz) shelled hazelnuts, roughly
    chopped and tossed in icing sugar

Preparation time: 1 hour
Cooking time: 35–40 minutes
Oven: 180°C, 350°F, Gas Mark 4

1. Line the bottoms of two greased 20cm
(8 inch) sandwich tins with non-stick silicone
paper or greased greaseproof paper.
2. Whisk the egg whites until stiff, then whisk
in the sugar a little at a time until thick and
glossy. Fold in the vanilla essence and
hazelnuts.
3. Divide the meringue equally between the
prepared tins and level the top. Bake in a
preheated oven for 35–40 minutes until the
meringue is crisp and lightly coloured on top.
Turn out of the tins on to a wire rack, carefully
peel off the lining paper and leave to cool.
4. Meanwhile, make the filling: beat the
chestnut purée with the icing sugar and rum
until smooth. Whip the cream until it holds its
shape, then fold into the chestnut mixture.
5. Place one round of meringue on a serving
plate, soft side uppermost, and spread with half
the filling. Place the remaining round of
meringue on top, crisp side uppermost, and
spread the remaining filling over the centre.
6. To finish, whip the cream until it holds its
shape and pipe rosettes of cream around the
edge of the cake. Sprinkle the chocolate over the
cream rosettes and sprinkle the sugared
hazelnuts over the filling in the centre. Serve as
soon as possible.

Serves 6

Nutrition content per serving   Carbohydrate: 67g   Fat: 35g
Fibre: 4g   Kilocalories: 597

SAVARIN WITH FRUITS

15g (½oz) fresh yeast
3 tablespoons lukewarm milk
100g (4oz) strong white flour
pinch of salt
1 teaspoon sugar
2 eggs, beaten
50g (2oz) butter, softened
mixed fresh fruit, such as halved strawberries,
    halved and pipped grapes, sliced kiwi fruit, etc.,
    to fill
SUGAR SYRUP:
225g (8oz) sugar
300ml (½ pint) water
4 tablespoons Kirsch, or to taste

Preparation time: 45 minutes, plus rising
Cooking time: 25–30 minutes
Oven: 200°C, 400°F, Gas Mark 6

1. Butter and flour a 20cm (8 inch) savarin or
ring mould.
2. Cream the yeast in a bowl with the lukewarm
milk, then gradually work in 25g (1oz) flour.
Leave to stand in a warm place for about 20
minutes until frothy, then add the remaining
flour, the salt, sugar, eggs and butter. Beat until
an elastic dough forms.
3. Put the dough into the mould, then leave in a
warm place for 45 minutes until the dough has
risen almost to the top of the mould.
4. Bake in a preheated oven for 25–30 minutes
or until the savarin is golden and has shrunk
away slightly from the sides of the mould.
5. Meanwhile, make the sugar syrup. Put the
sugar and water in a heavy pan and bring to the
boil, stirring occasionally. Simmer without
stirring for 5 minutes until syrupy. Remove
from the heat and stir in the Kirsch.
6. Unmould the savarin and place it the right
way up on a wire rack placed over a tray. Prick
all over with a fine skewer, then slowly spoon
over the hot sugar syrup. Continue spooning the
syrup over the savarin until the cake becomes
saturated, using the syrup that drips into the
tray underneath. Leave to cool.
7. Mix the fruit with the sugar syrup which has
collected in the tray. Place the savarin on a
serving plate, spoon the fruit into the centre and
serve immediately.

Serves 6

Nutrition content per serving   Carbohydrate: 64g   Fat: 9g
Fibre: 3g   Kilocalories: 362

TOP: Chestnut Vacherin; BOTTOM: Savarin with Fruits.

FROSTED COFFEE CAKE

175g (6oz) butter, softened
175g (6oz) caster sugar
3 eggs, beaten
175g (6oz) self-raising flour
2 tablespoons strong black coffee
ICING:
225g (8oz) icing sugar, sifted
50g (2oz) butter
2 tablespoons strong black coffee

Preparation time: 20 minutes
Cooking time: 30 minutes
Oven: 180°C, 350°F, Gas Mark 4

1. Grease two 20cm (8 inch) round sandwich tins and line the bottoms with greased greaseproof paper.
2. Place the butter and sugar in a bowl and beat until the mixture is light and fluffy, scraping down the sides of the bowl at intervals.
3. Add the beaten eggs a little at a time, beating well between each addition.
4. Add the flour and fold in lightly with a metal spoon, cutting through the mixture and turning it over until the flour is evenly mixed. Lightly fold in the coffee.
5. Divide the mixture between the prepared tins. Level the tops with the back of a metal spoon.
6. Bake in a preheated oven for 30 minutes until the cakes are golden brown and spring back when pressed with the fingers.
7. Turn out the cakes, remove the lining paper and cool on a wire rack.
8. To make the icing, place the icing ingredients in a bowl over a saucepan of hot water. Heat gently, stirring until smooth and glossy. Remove the pan from the heat.
9. Leave the icing until it is cold, then beat until thick enough to spread.
10. Place one cake on a serving plate. Spread with half the icing. Cover with the other cake. Spread the top with the remaining icing, swirling with a round-ended knife.

Serves 6–8

Nutrition content per serving   Carbohydrate: 93–69g
Fat: 34–26g   Fibre: 1g   Kilocalories: 679–509

CZECHOSLOVAKIAN CURD CHEESECAKE

100g (4oz) shelled walnuts or hazelnuts
75g (3oz) fine white breadcrumbs
100g (4oz) unsalted butter, softened
100g (4oz) caster sugar
4 eggs, separated
100g (4oz) curd cheese, sieved or beaten until smooth in a food processor
TO FINISH:
2–3 tablespoons apricot jam, heated and sieved
25–50g (1–2oz) chopped walnuts or hazelnuts
25–50g (1–2oz) grated chocolate

Preparation time: 20–25 minutes
Cooking time: 50–60 minutes
Oven: 180°C, 350°F, Gas Mark 4

1. Place the nuts on a baking sheet and bake in a preheated oven for 12–15 minutes until golden brown. Turn the nuts occasionally so that they colour evenly. Remove the skins from the hazelnuts, if using. Chop or crush the nuts coarsely.
2. Line the bottom and sides of a 20cm (8 inch) springform or loose-bottomed cake tin with buttered greaseproof paper and sprinkle lightly with some of the breadcrumbs.
3. Cream the butter and sugar together until light and fluffy. Beat in the egg yolks one at a time, then add the cheese and beat thoroughly.
4. Whisk the egg whites until stiff and fold in gently with the remaining breadcrumbs and the nuts.
5. Place the mixture in the prepared tin and bake in a preheated oven for 40–45 minutes until the top feels springy and the cake starts to shrink away from the sides of the tin.
6. Remove from the oven but leave in the tin until cold.
7. Turn out the cheesecake carefully. When ready to serve, spread the hot jam over the top, sprinkle with the nuts and when the jam has cooled, sprinkle with the grated chocolate.

Serves 6–8

Nutrition content per serving   Carbohydrate: 34–25g
Fat: 32–24g   Fibre: 2–1g   Kilocalories: 457–343

TOP: Frosted Coffee Cake; BOTTOM: Czechoslovakian Curd Cheesecake.

PASSION CAKE

150g (5oz) butter
200g (7oz) soft light brown sugar
175g (6oz) grated carrots
½ teaspoon salt
1 teaspoon ground mixed spice
2 eggs
200g (7oz) self-raising flour
2 teaspoons baking powder
100g (4oz) shelled walnuts, finely chopped
ICING:
225g (8oz) full fat soft cheese
2–3 tablespoons lemon juice
50g (2oz) icing sugar, sifted
25g (1oz) shelled walnuts, chopped, to finish

Preparation time: 20 minutes
Cooking time: 1 hour
Oven: 180°C, 350°F, Gas Mark 4

1. Grease a 20cm (8 inch) round cake tin and line with greased greaseproof paper.
2. Melt the butter and pour into a mixing bowl. Beat in the sugar, carrots, salt, spice and eggs.
3. Sift the flour and baking powder together and add the walnuts. Fold into the carrot mixture lightly until evenly mixed.
4. Pour the mixture into the prepared tin. Bake in a preheated oven for 1 hour, until firm to the touch and golden brown.
5. Cool in the tin for 5 minutes, then turn out and cool completely on a wire rack.
6. Beat the cheese until smooth. Gradually beat in the lemon juice according to taste, then beat in the icing sugar until well mixed.
7. Split the cake into two layers and sandwich with one-third of the icing. Spread the remaining icing over the top and sides of the cake, marking with a fork.
8. Sprinkle the top edge of the cake with the chopped walnuts.

Variation: Bake the cake mixture in paper cake cases to make small passion cakes. The above quantity will make about 24 cakes. Half fill the cases, then bake for 20–25 minutes. When cool, spread them with the cheese icing and top each with a walnut half.

Serves 8

Nutrition content per serving   Carbohydrate: 55g   Fat: 39g
Fibre: 2g   Kilocalories: 579

SPICED SWISS ROLL

4 eggs
100g (4oz) caster sugar
100g (4oz) plain flour
¼ teaspoon ground mixed spice
½ teaspoon ground ginger
25g (1oz) butter, melted and cooled
icing sugar, to finish
FILLING:
100g (4oz) butter, softened
225g (8oz) icing sugar, sifted
1–2 teaspoons lemon juice
finely grated rind of ½ lemon
175–225g (6–8oz) ginger preserve

Preparation time: 40 minutes
Cooking time: 15–20 minutes
Oven: 190°C, 375°F, Gas Mark 5

1. Grease a 30 × 25cm (12 × 10 inch) Swiss roll tin and line with greased greaseproof paper.
2. Put the eggs and sugar into a large heatproof bowl and place over a saucepan of gently simmering water; whisk until the mixture is thick and pale. (If a large electric mixer is used, no heat is required.)
3. Sift the flour and spices together twice and fold quickly and evenly through the whisked mixture using a metal spoon.
4. Finally fold the butter through the mixture and turn quickly into the tin, spreading out to ensure that the corners are well filled.
5. Place in a preheated oven and bake for 15–20 minutes or until a pale golden brown and just firm and springy to the touch.
6. Turn the sponge out on to a sheet of greaseproof paper or non-stick silicone paper lightly dredged with caster sugar. Peel off the lining paper carefully, trim the edges with a knife and roll up the cake quickly from a short end while still warm with the sugared paper inside. Cool on a wire rack.
7. For the filling: cream the butter and icing sugar together and add the lemon juice a few drops at a time until a spreading consistency is obtained. Add the lemon rind.
8. Unroll the cake carefully and remove the paper. Spread first all over with ginger preserve and then with the filling. Reroll the cake carefully and dredge with sifted icing sugar.

Serves 6

Nutrition content per serving   Carbohydrate: 97g   Fat: 21g
Fibre: 1g   Kilocalories: 578

TOP: Passion Cake; BOTTOM: Spiced Swiss Roll.

HAZELNUT CREAM ROULADE

3 eggs
75g (3oz) plus 3 tablespoons caster sugar
75g (3oz) shelled hazelnuts, freshly ground
2 tablespoons wholemeal flour
300ml ($\frac{1}{2}$ pint) whipping cream, whipped
225g (8oz) fresh blackberries

Preparation time: 25 minutes
Cooking time: 20 minutes
Oven: 200°C, 400°F, Gas Mark 6

1. Grease a 33 × 23cm (13 × 9 inch) Swiss roll tin and line with greased greaseproof paper.
2. Whisk the eggs and 75g (3oz) of the sugar in a basin over hot water until thick and pale. (No heat is needed if using an electric mixer.)
3. Off the heat, fold in the hazelnuts and flour with a metal spoon. Spread the mixture evenly in the prepared tin and bake in a preheated oven for about 10 minutes until firm and golden.
4. Sprinkle a large piece of greaseproof paper with 2 tablespoons caster sugar. Turn the hazelnut cake on to the paper, remove the lining paper very carefully and, starting at a short end, roll up the cake with the greaseproof paper inside it. Allow to cool on a wire rack.
5. Unroll the cake carefully and spread with three-quarters of the cream. Arrange three-quarters of the blackberries on top and roll up again. Sprinkle with the remaining sugar. Trim the ends and transfer to a serving plate.

6. Decorate with whirls of the remaining cream and the remaining blackberries.

Serves 6

Nutrition content per serving   Carbohydrate: 21g   Fat: 32g
Fibre: 4g   Kilocalories: 386

CHOCOLATE ANGEL FOOD

25g (1oz) plain flour, sifted
25g (1oz) cocoa powder, sifted
120g (4 $\frac{1}{2}$ oz) caster sugar
5 egg whites
pinch of salt
$\frac{1}{2}$ teaspoon cream of tartar
TO FINISH:
icing sugar
grated plain chocolate
chocolate ice cream or whipped cream, to serve

Preparation time: 20 minutes
Cooking time: 30–40 minutes
Oven: 180°C, 350°F, Gas Mark 4

1. Lightly flour, but do not butter, an 18cm (7 inch) springform cake tin, using the base with the central funnel. Sift the flour, cocoa powder and 75g (3oz) of the sugar together three times.
2. Whisk the egg whites with the salt in a mixing bowl until foamy and add the cream of tartar. Continue whisking until the egg whites form stiff peaks. Add the remaining sugar, beating until the egg whites are firm and glossy.
3. Sift the flour mixture over the egg whites and gently but thoroughly fold into the egg whites. Pour the mixture immediately into the tin. Bake in a preheated oven for 30–40 minutes or until a skewer comes out clean and the cake is springy to the touch.
4. Remove from the oven and invert the tin on to a wire rack. Leave the cake to cool completely, then run a knife around the sides and unmould from the tin. Dust with icing sugar and sprinkle with chocolate. Serve sliced, with ice cream or whipped cream.

Serves 4–6

Nutrition content per serving (excluding ice cream or cream)
Carbohydrate: 41–27g   Fat: 1g   Fibre: 0g   Kilocalories: 181–120

ABOVE: Hazelnut Cream Roulade.
RIGHT: Chocolate Angel Food.

CHOCOLATE RUM CAKE

225g (8oz) butter
225g (8oz) plain chocolate
100g (4oz) caster sugar
3 eggs
100g (4oz) maraschino cherries, well drained
100g (4oz) shelled mixed nuts (walnuts, toasted
   almonds and hazelnuts), roughly chopped
2 tablespoons dark rum
225g (8oz) plain sweet biscuits, roughly broken

Preparation time: 20 minutes
Cooking time: 5 minutes

1. Grease a 23 × 13cm (9 × 5 inch) loaf tin and
line the bottom with greaseproof paper.
2. Melt the butter and chocolate together in a
saucepan over gentle heat. Allow to cool.
3. Place the sugar and eggs in a bowl and whisk
together until pale and thick. Fold in the
chocolate mixture, and then add the remaining
ingredients. Spoon the mixture into the
prepared tin, cover and freeze.
4. To serve, unmould on to a serving plate and
allow to soften in the refrigerator for about 30
minutes. Cut into slices to serve.

Serves 12–14

Nutrition content per serving   Carbohydrate: 37–32g
Fat: 30–24g   Fibre: 1g   Kilocalories: 431–369

TOP: Chocolate Rum Cake; BOTTOM: Devil's Food
Cake.

DEVIL'S FOOD CAKE

75g (3oz) plain chocolate, broken into pieces
175ml (6fl oz) strong black coffee
175g (6oz) unsalted butter
225g (8oz) soft dark brown sugar
50g (2oz) vanilla sugar
3 eggs
275g (10oz) plain flour
1½ teaspoons bicarbonate of soda
175ml (6fl oz) soured cream
ICING:
450g (1 lb) sugar
300ml (½ pint) water
2 egg whites, stiffly whisked

Preparation time: 35 minutes
Cooking time: 45–50 minutes
Oven: 190°C, 375°F, Gas Mark 5

1. Butter three 20cm (8 inch) sandwich tins and
line with greaseproof paper. Brush the paper
with melted butter and dust with flour.
2. Place the chocolate in a saucepan with the
coffee and stir over a low heat until the
chocolate melts. Leave to cool.
3. Beat the butter in a mixing bowl until pale
and soft. Add the sugars and beat until fluffy.
Add the eggs one at a time, beating well after
each addition. Stir in the chocolate. Sift the
flour and bicarbonate of soda together and fold
into the chocolate mixture alternating, in two or
three additions, with the soured cream.
4. Divide the mixture between the tins and bake
in a preheated oven for 25 minutes or until a
skewer inserted into the centre comes out clean.
Remove from the oven and leave in the tins for
5 minutes before turning out to cool completely.
5. To make the icing, place the sugar and water
in a heavy saucepan and stir over a medium heat
until the sugar dissolves. Brush away any sugar
crystals that have formed on the sides of the pan
with a pastry brush dipped in cold water.
Increase the heat and bring to the boil. Cook to
the soft-ball stage, 115°C (238°F). Remove from
the heat and dip the base in cold water to arrest
further cooking. Gradually beat the syrup into
the whisked egg whites. Continue beating until
the icing thickens and loses its sheen. Use
immediately to sandwich the cake layers and
spread over the top and sides.

Serves 6–8

Nutrition content per serving   Carbohydrate: 173–129g
Fat: 37–28g   Fibre: 2–1g   Kilocalories: 1024–768

Small cakes

◆

& BARS

These toothsome delicacies are welcome at any time – with tea or coffee, as a snack, in a packed lunch or on a picnic, or even as a dessert.
Many of the recipes in this chapter will be particularly appealing to children, perhaps because they are just the right size for little fingers. Lightly spiced buns filled with jam or lemon curd and sprinkled with sugar, and Queen Cakes, baked in individual paper cases and topped with glacé icing and cherries, are just two to choose from.
Oats and nuts give a delicious chewy texture to several of these bars and fingers. Others are iced or glazed for a decorative finish.

Gingerbread Fingers; Frosted Orange Squares
(see recipes on page 58).

FROSTED ORANGE SQUARES

225g (8oz) butter, melted, or 250ml (8fl oz)
    vegetable oil
300ml (½ pint) unsweetened orange juice
275g (10oz) caster sugar
2 eggs, beaten
400g (14oz) self-raising flour
ICING:
100g (4oz) icing sugar, sifted
3 tablespoons unsweetened orange juice

Preparation time: 10 minutes
Cooking time: 1 hour
Oven: 180°C, 350°F, Gas Mark 4

1. Grease a 20 × 25cm (8 × 10 inch) tin and line the bottom with greased greaseproof paper.
2. Place all the cake ingredients in a bowl. Beat well until smooth and evenly mixed.
3. Pour into the tin and bake in a preheated oven for 1 hour, until firm and golden brown.
4. To make the icing, place the sugar and orange juice in a bowl and beat until smooth. Pour over the warm cake and leave to cool.
5. When cold, cut into 5cm (2 inch) squares.

Makes 20

Nutrition content per serving   Carbohydrate: 37g   Fat: 10g
Fibre: 1g   Kilocalories: 239

GINGERBREAD FINGERS

100g (4oz) butter
100g (4oz) Muscovado raw cane sugar
250ml (8fl oz) black treacle
225g (8oz) plain flour
½ teaspoon bicarbonate of soda
5cm (2 inch) fresh root ginger, peeled and grated
1 tablespoon ground ginger
1 tablespoon ground cinnamon
2 tablespoons plain unsweetened yogurt
2 tablespoons orange juice
2 eggs (size 1), lightly beaten

Preparation time: 20 minutes, plus cooling, then 2 days storing
Cooking time: 35–40 minutes
Oven: 160°C, 325°F, Gas Mark 3

1. Put the butter, sugar and treacle into a saucepan and heat gently, stirring occasionally, until melted and smooth. Remove from the heat and leave to cool for about 5 minutes.
2. Meanwhile, sift the flour into a large bowl with the bicarbonate of soda, then add the grated ginger, the ground ginger and cinnamon.
3. Stir the yogurt into the treacle mixture, then add the orange juice and eggs and whisk well.
4. Add the liquid mixture to the sifted flour and stir for 3–4 minutes to make sure the treacle and flour are completely blended.
5. Pour the mixture into a greased shallow baking tin, 30 × 25cm (12 × 10 inches). Bake in a preheated oven for 35–40 minutes or until springy when pressed. Leave to cool.
6. Cut the cake in half, then cut each half into fingers 2.5cm (1 inch) in width. Lift out of the tin and store in an airtight container for 2 days before eating.

Makes 20–24

Nutrition content per serving   Carbohydrate: 23–19g   Fat: 5–4g
Fibre: 0g   Kilocalories: 138–115

BROWN SUGAR MERINGUES

100g (4oz) caster sugar
100g (4oz) soft light brown sugar
4 egg whites
300ml (½ pint) whipping cream, whipped

Preparation time: about 15 minutes
Cooking time: about 2 hours
Oven: 120°C, 250°F, Gas Mark ½

1. Line two baking sheets with non-stick silicone paper. Sift the sugars together twice.
2. Put the egg whites in a grease-free bowl and whisk until stiff, dry and standing in peaks. Whisk in the sugars a little at a time.
3. Put the meringue mixture into a piping bag fitted with a star vegetable nozzle. Pipe into fingers or whirls on the baking sheet.
4. Bake in a preheated oven for about 2 hours, reversing the baking sheets after an hour, until the meringues are firm and dry and may easily be moved from the paper. Leave to cool.
5. Sandwich the meringues together with cream. Serve with raspberries or other fruit.

Makes about 20

Nutrition content per serving   Carbohydrate: 11g   Fat: 5g
Fibre: 0g   Kilocalories: 92

Brown Sugar Meringues.

HAZELNUT TEACAKES

100g (4oz) wholewheat flour
1 teaspoon light muscovado sugar
1 tablespoon dried yeast
175ml (6fl oz) lukewarm milk
DOUGH:
350g (12oz) wholewheat flour
pinch of salt
50g (2oz) butter, softened
3 tablespoons clear honey, melted
75g (3oz) shelled hazelnuts, chopped
1 egg, beaten
GLAZE:
1 tablespoon milk
1 tablespoon light muscovado sugar

Preparation time: 30 minutes, plus standing and rising
Cooking time: 25 minutes
Oven: 220°C, 425°F, Gas Mark 7

1. Mix together the flour, sugar and dried yeast, pour on the milk and mix to a smooth batter. Set aside in a warm place for about 15 minutes until the mixture is frothy.
2. To make the dough, sift the flour and salt into a mixing bowl and rub in the butter using a fork. Stir in the honey, nuts and egg. Pour on the yeast batter mixture and mix until the dough leaves the sides of the bowl.
3. Turn out the dough on to a lightly floured board and knead for about 10 minutes, or until it is smooth and pliable. Shape the dough into a ball, return it to the bowl and cover with a piece of oiled polythene. Leave it in a warm place for about 45 minutes, or until it has doubled in size.
4. Knead the dough lightly and divide it into 8 equal pieces. Shape the dough into rounds and place them well apart on two baking sheets.
5. Bake the teacakes in a preheated oven for 20 minutes, or until they sound hollow when tapped underneath. Mix together the milk and sugar for the glaze, brush it over the teacakes and return them to the oven for 2–3 minutes. Serve warm, split and filled with honey and soft cheese, or split and toasted.

Makes 8

Nutrition content per serving   Carbohydrate: 46g   Fat: 11g
Fibre: 6g   Kilocalories: 312

TOP: Iced Finger Fancies; BOTTOM: Hazelnut Teacakes.

ICED FINGER FANCIES

150g (6oz) self-raising flour
1½ teaspoons baking powder
150g (6oz) soft tub margarine
150g (6oz) caster or light soft brown sugar
3 eggs (size 1 or 2)
2 tablespoons sifted cocoa blended with
    2 tablespoons hot water, or 1½ tablespoons
    instant coffee powder sifted with the flour, or
    the grated rind of 1½ lemons or oranges,
    or ½ teaspoon almond essence
BUTTERCREAM:
175g (6oz) butter
275–350g (10–12oz) icing sugar, sifted
vanilla essence or other flavouring
2–3 tablespoons milk
liquid food colouring
TO DECORATE (A SELECTION OF):
glacé cherries, chopped toasted nuts, chocolate
    buttons, matchsticks or crumbled chocolate flake
    bar, jellied fruit slices, pistachio nuts, walnut or
    pecan halves, toasted blanched almonds, angelica

Preparation time: about 1 hour
Cooking time: 40–45 minutes
Oven: 160°C, 325°F, Gas Mark 3

1. Grease a rectangular tin about 28 × 18 × 4cm (11 × 7 × 1½ inches) and line with greased greaseproof paper.
2. Sift the flour and baking powder into a bowl and add the margarine, sugar, eggs and one of the flavourings. Beat until smooth.
3. Turn the mixture into the tin, making sure there is plenty in the corners, and bake in a preheated oven for 40–45 minutes or until well risen and firm to the touch. Cool on a wire rack, then peel off the paper.
4. To make the buttercream, beat the butter until soft, then gradually beat in the sugar with the flavouring and milk to make a firm but spreadable consistency. Colour to suit the cake.
5. Spread a thinnish layer over the top of the cake. Put the remainder into a piping bag fitted with a star or thick writing nozzle. Decorate the top of the icing with piping. Add decoration of choice and leave to set. Cut first down the centre and then cut each bar into fingers between the decorations. Or, cut into bars before adding the final decorations.

Makes 14–16

Nutrition content per serving   Carbohydrate: 43–38g
Fat: 21–18g   Fibre: 0g   Kilocalories: 363–317

GREEK CITRUS DIAMONDS

100g (4oz) butter, softened
225g (8oz) caster sugar
175g (6oz) plain flour
2 teaspoons baking powder
pinch of salt
½ teaspoon ground mixed spice
50g (2oz) fine semolina
finely grated rind and juice of 2 oranges
2 eggs
1 tablespoon sesame seeds
SYRUP GLAZE:
100g (4oz) sugar
finely grated rind and juice of 1 orange
2 tablespoons clear honey
TO DECORATE:
2 tablespoons sesame seeds
lightly toasted strips of candied orange peel

Preparation time: 30–40 minutes
Cooking time: about 1 hour 20 minutes
Oven: 180°C, 350°F, Gas Mark 4

1. Grease a 25 × 18cm (10 × 7 inch) tin and line with greased greaseproof paper or non-stick silicone paper.
2. Cream the butter and sugar together until pale and fluffy; this can be done by hand, with an electric mixer or in a food processor.
3. Sift together the flour, baking powder, salt and mixed spice. Add to the creamed mixture, together with the semolina, orange rind and juice, eggs and sesame seeds. Mix well until blended.
4. Spread the mixture evenly in the prepared tin and bake in a preheated oven for about 1¼ hours, until firm but spongy to the touch.
5. Meanwhile make the syrup glaze. Put the sugar and orange rind and juice into a pan and stir over a gentle heat until the sugar has dissolved. Add the honey and boil gently for 3 minutes.
6. When the cake is ready, remove it from the oven and pierce it at evenly-spaced intervals with a fine skewer. Spoon the syrup glaze evenly over the top.
7. Sprinkle with the toasted sesame seeds. Leave to cool.
8. Decorate with the strips of candied orange peel. Cut into diamond shapes and serve.

Makes 8–10

Nutrition content per serving   Carbohydrate: 73–59g
Fat: 13–11g   Fibre: 1g   Kilocalories: 414–331

CINNAMON ALMOND SLICES

100g (4oz) butter, softened
50g (2oz) caster sugar
150g (6oz) plain flour
½ teaspoon ground cinnamon
a little beaten egg, to glaze
25g (1oz) flaked or nibbed almonds
1 tablespoon granulated sugar

Preparation time: 30 minutes
Cooking time: 20 minutes
Oven: 180°C, 350°F, Gas Mark 4

1. Well grease a 28 × 18cm (11 × 7 inch) Swiss roll tin.
2. Cream the butter and sugar together until light and fluffy. Sift in the flour and cinnamon and work well together.
3. Press into the prepared tin and flatten with a palette knife. Brush with a little beaten egg and prick with a fork. Sprinkle over the almonds and sugar.
4. Bake in a preheated oven for 20 minutes or until golden brown. Cool in the tin and mark into 18 fingers while still warm.

Makes 18

Nutrition content per serving   Carbohydrate: 11g   Fat: 6g
Fibre: 0g   Kilocalories: 94

TOP: Greek Citrus Diamonds; BOTTOM: Cinnamon Almond Slices.

JAMMY BUNS

225g (8oz) self-raising flour
pinch of salt
pinch of ground mixed spice
50g (2oz) butter
50g (2oz) caster sugar
1 egg, beaten
2 tablespoons milk
2 tablespoons jam or lemon curd
1 tablespoon granulated sugar

Preparation time: 25 minutes
Cooking time: 10 minutes
Oven: 220°C, 425°F, Gas Mark 7

1. Sift the flour, salt and mixed spice into a bowl and rub in the butter with the fingertips until the mixture resembles fine crumbs. Stir in the caster sugar, and add the egg and enough milk to make a firm dough. Knead lightly until smooth.
2. Divide the dough into 12 pieces and roll them into balls. Make a hole in each bun and place ½ teaspoon of jam in each one, then pinch the opening together firmly and place the buns, jam side down, on a greased baking sheet.
3. Sprinkle the tops of the buns with the granulated sugar and bake in a preheated oven for 10 minutes or until brown. Cool on a wire rack.

Makes 12

Nutrition content per serving   Carbohydrate: 22g   Fat: 4g
Fibre: 1g   Kilocalories: 131

CHOCOLATE TOFFEE BARS

175g (6oz) butter, softened
75g (3oz) caster sugar
250g (9oz) plain flour
TOPPING:
100g (4oz) butter
50g (2oz) caster sugar
2 tablespoons golden syrup
1 × 200g (7oz) can condensed milk
100g (4oz) plain or milk chocolate

Preparation time: 25 minutes, plus cooling
Cooking time: 35 minutes
Oven: 160°C, 325°F, Gas Mark 3

1. To make the biscuit base, place the butter

and sugar in a bowl and beat until light and fluffy.
2. Add the flour and mix to a soft dough.
3. Knead the dough lightly on a floured surface, then roll out and line the bottom of an 18 × 28cm (7 × 11 inch) shallow tin.
4. Bake in a preheated oven for 35 minutes, until just beginning to colour. Leave to cool in the tin.
5. To make the topping, place the butter, sugar, syrup and condensed milk in a heavy-based saucepan. Heat gently until the sugar has dissolved, then boil for 5 minutes, stirring until toffee-coloured and thickened.
6. Cool slightly, then spread over the biscuit base. Leave until cold.
7. Break up the chocolate and place in a bowl over a saucepan of hot water until it has melted.
8. Spread the chocolate evenly over the toffee, making wavy lines with a round-ended knife.
9. Leave to set, then cut into three lengthways and eight across.

Makes 24

Nutrition content per serving   Carbohydrate: 22g   Fat: 11g
Fibre: 0g   Kilocalories: 194

ABOVE: Jammy Buns.
LEFT: Chocolate Toffee Bars

BROWNIES

100g (4oz) butter
100g (4oz) plain chocolate, broken into pieces
100g (4oz) soft brown sugar
100g (4oz) self-raising flour
pinch of salt
2 eggs, beaten
50g (2oz) shelled walnuts, coarsely chopped
1–2 tablespoons milk

Preparation time: 25 minutes
Cooking time: about 30 minutes
Oven: 180°C, 350°F, Gas Mark 4

1. Grease a 20cm (8 inch) square cake tin.
2. Put the butter and chocolate pieces in a heatproof bowl and warm over a pan of hot water until melted, stirring occasionally. Remove the bowl from the heat. Stir in the sugar and mix thoroughly. Leave to cool.
3. Sift the flour and salt into a mixing bowl. Make a well in the centre and pour in the cooled chocolate mixture. Mix together. Beat in the eggs and walnuts, then add enough milk to make a soft dropping consistency.
4. Pour into the tin and bake in a preheated oven for about 30 minutes or until a skewer inserted in the centre comes out clean. Leave to cool in the tin before cutting into squares.

Makes about 16

Nutrition content per serving   Carbohydrate: 16g   Fat: 9g
Fibre: 0g   Kilocalories: 153

ICED WALNUT SQUARES

3 eggs, separated
100g (4oz) caster sugar
100g (4oz) shelled walnuts, ground
1 teaspoon plain flour, sifted
TO FINISH:
100g (4oz) icing sugar, sifted
2 teaspoons lemon juice
16 walnut halves, to decorate

Preparation time: 30 minutes
Cooking time: 25–30 minutes
Oven: 150°C, 300°F, Gas Mark 2

1. Grease and flour a 20cm (8 inch) square tin.
2. Beat the egg yolks with the sugar until thick and light in colour. Stir in the ground walnuts

and flour. Whisk the egg whites until stiff and standing in peaks. Fold into the nut mixture.
3. Spread the mixture in the tin. Place in a preheated oven and bake for 25–30 minutes until set and lightly coloured. Remove from the tin and cool on a wire rack.
4. Place the icing sugar in a bowl and stir in sufficient lemon juice to give a smooth consistency. Spread this over the top of the cake. Cut into squares and decorate each one with a walnut half while the icing is still soft. Allow the icing to set before serving.

Makes 16

Nutrition content per serving   Carbohydrate: 14g   Fat: 5g
Fibre: 0g   Kilocalories: 108

PEACH & OAT FINGERS

100g (4oz) butter
100g (4oz) caster sugar
100g (4oz) self-raising flour
pinch of bicarbonate of soda
100g (4oz) rolled oats
1 egg, beaten
2 ripe peaches, skinned and sliced

Preparation time: 15 minutes
Cooking time: 40–45 minutes
Oven: 190°C, 375°F, Gas Mark 5

1. Grease an 18cm (7 inch) square cake tin and line with greased greaseproof paper. Melt the butter in a pan. Add the sugar and stir well until the sugar has melted.
2. Sift in the flour and bicarbonate of soda, then stir in the rolled oats.
3. Cool slightly then beat in the egg.
4. Place half of the cake mixture in the prepared tin and arrange the peaches on top, pressing the slices down lightly. Top with the remaining mixture, spreading it gently over the peaches.
5. Place in a preheated oven and cook for 35–40 minutes. Cool slightly in the tin then cut into fingers. Transfer to a wire rack to cool.

Makes about 14

Nutrition content per serving   Carbohydrate: 20g   Fat: 6g
Fibre: 1g   Kilocalories: 150

FROM TOP TO BOTTOM: Brownies; Iced Walnut Squares; Peach & Oat Fingers.

YOGURT & HONEY CAKES

4 eggs, separated
225g (8oz) caster sugar
100g (4oz) butter, melted
200ml (7fl oz) plain unsweetened yogurt
¼ teaspoon bicarbonate of soda
275g (10oz) plain flour
1 tablespoon baking powder
100g (4oz) clear honey
4 tablespoons water
strip of lemon rind
cinnamon stick
50g (2oz) flaked almonds, toasted

Preparation time: 15 minutes
Cooking time: 25 minutes
Oven: 190°C, 375°F, Gas Mark 5

1. Grease a 33 × 23cm (13 × 9 inch) shallow tin.
2. Place the egg yolks and sugar in a bowl and whisk either by hand over a pan of simmering water, or using an electric whisk on high speed, until light and thick, about 5 minutes.
3. Whisk in the melted butter. Mix together the yogurt and bicarbonate of soda and stir in.
4. Whisk the egg whites until stiff. Fold lightly into the mixture with a metal spoon.
5. Sift the flour and baking powder into the bowl and fold in lightly until well mixed.
6. Pour the mixture into the prepared tin and smooth the top.
7. Bake in a preheated oven for 25 minutes until the cake is golden brown and springs back when pressed with the fingers. Leave to cool in the tin.
8. Place the honey, water, lemon rind and cinnamon stick in a saucepan. Heat gently for 5 minutes.
9. Remove the lemon rind and cinnamon stick and pour the syrup evenly over the cake. Sprinkle with the almonds.
10. Leave until the syrup is cold, then cut the cake into three lengthways and eight across.

Makes 24

Nutrition content per serving   Carbohydrate: 23g   Fat: 6g
Fibre: 1g   Kilocalories: 149

MUNCHY DATE LAYER FINGERS

FILLING:
225g (8oz) dates, stoned and chopped
2 tablespoons water
1 tablespoon lemon juice
1 tablespoon honey
pinch of ground cinnamon
OAT MIXTURE:
100g (4oz) wholemeal flour
175g (6oz) rolled oats
225g (8oz) butter

Preparation time: 20 minutes
Cooking time: 35–40 minutes
Oven: 180°C, 350°F, Gas Mark 4

1. Put the dates and water in a pan and simmer gently until the dates are soft. Allow to cool, then stir in the lemon juice, honey and cinnamon.
2. Well grease an 18 cm (7 inch) shallow square cake tin.
3. Mix the flour and oats in a mixing bowl. Rub in the butter. Divide this mixture in half. Press half into the bottom of the prepared tin. Spread with the date mixture and cover with the remaining oat mixture.
4. Bake in a preheated oven for 20–25 minutes. Cool in the tin and cut into fingers while still warm. Remove from the tin carefully when quite cold.

Makes 14

Nutrition content per serving   Carbohydrate: 25g   Fat: 14g
Fibre: 3g   Kilocalories: 235

TOP: Yogurt & Honey Cakes; BOTTOM: Munchy Date Layer Fingers.

CRUMBLE FRUIT BARS

225g (8oz) mixed dried fruit (e.g. peaches, pears,
*   apples, bananas, dates, figs), chopped*
300ml ($\frac{1}{2}$ pint) water
150ml ($\frac{1}{4}$ pint) orange juice
150g (6oz) plain flour
100g (4oz) semolina
100g (4oz) butter
75g (3oz) caster sugar
granulated sugar, for sprinkling

Preparation time: 15 minutes
Cooking time: about 1 hour
Oven: 190°C, 375°F, Gas Mark 5

1. Place the dried fruit, water and orange juice in a saucepan. Bring to the boil, then reduce the heat, cover and cook gently for 30 minutes. Leave to cool.
2. Place the flour and semolina in a bowl. Add the butter, cut into pieces, and rub in until the mixture resembles fine breadcrumbs. Stir in the caster sugar.
3. Sprinkle half the crumble evenly over the bottom of a 28 × 18cm (11 × 7 inch) shallow tin. Carefully spread the fruit over the top and sprinkle with the remaining crumble. Press down lightly.
4. Bake in a preheated oven for 30–35 minutes, until pale golden. Sprinkle with granulated sugar and leave in the tin until cold. Cut in half

down the length, then into eight across to make into bars.

Variation: Replace the dried fruit with chopped dates and add the grated rind and juice of 1 lemon.

Makes 16

Nutrition content per serving   Carbohydrate: 28g   Fat: 5g
Fibre: 2g   Kilocalories: 160

QUEEN CAKES

100g (4oz) butter, softened
100g (4oz) caster sugar
2 eggs, beaten
100g (4oz) self-raising flour
$\frac{1}{2}$ teaspoon vanilla essence
50g (2oz) sultanas, chopped
1–2 tablespoons milk
TO FINISH:
150g (5oz) icing sugar, sifted
2–3 tablespoons warm water
10 glacé cherries, halved

Preparation time: 30 minutes
Cooking time: 15 minutes
Oven: 180°C, 350°F, Gas Mark 4

1. Cream the butter and sugar together until very pale and fluffy. Gradually beat in the eggs, the equivalent of one at a time, adding a little flour between each addition. Stir in the vanilla essence and sultanas. Fold in the remaining flour, adding sufficient milk to make a soft dropping consistency.
2. Divide the mixture equally between 20 paper cases and bake in a preheated oven for 15 minutes or until the cakes spring back when lightly pressed. Allow the cakes to cool on a wire rack.
3. To finish, mix the icing sugar with enough water to make a smooth thick icing. Use to ice each cake, and gently press half a glacé cherry on the top.

Makes 20

Nutrition content per serving   Carbohydrate: 19g   Fat: 5g
Fibre: 0g   Kilocalories: 120

ABOVE: Crumble Fruit Bars.
RIGHT: Queen Cakes.

FLORENTINE SLICES

*225g (8oz) block plain chocolate, broken into
  pieces*
50g (2oz) butter
100g (4oz) demerara sugar
1 egg, beaten
50g (2oz) mixed dried fruit
100g (4oz) sweetened desiccated coconut
*50g (2oz) chopped mixed peel or glacé cherries,
  quartered*

Preparation time: 25 minutes
Cooking time: 40–45 minutes
Oven: 150°C, 300°F, Gas Mark 2

1. Put the chocolate pieces in a heatproof bowl
and place over a pan of hot water until melted,
stirring occasionally. Spoon the chocolate into
a greased 19cm (7½ inch) square cake tin.
Spread it out evenly over the bottom and leave
to set.
2. Meanwhile, cream together the butter and
sugar until the mixture is light and fluffy. Beat
in the egg thoroughly. Mix together the
remaining ingredients and add to the creamed
mixture. Spoon into the tin and spread over the
set chocolate.
3. Bake in the centre of a preheated oven for
40–45 minutes, or until golden brown. Remove
from the oven and leave for 5 minutes, then
carefully mark into 12–16 squares with a sharp
knife. The mixture will be quite sticky at this
stage.
4. Leave until cold, then loosen with a palette
knife and lift each square carefully from the tin
so as not to mark the chocolate.

Makes 12–16

Nutrition content per serving   Carbohydrate: 28–21g
Fat: 14–10g   Fibre: 2–1g   Kilocalories: 235–177

CRUNCHY MUESLI BARS

4 tablespoons vegetable oil
6 tablespoons honey
25g (1oz) light muscovado sugar
150g (6oz) porridge oats
50g (2oz) sunflower seeds
25g (1oz) sesame seeds
25g (1oz) desiccated coconut
50g (2oz) dried apricot pieces, chopped
50g (2oz) sultanas

Preparation time: 10 minutes
Cooking time: 20–25 minutes
Oven: 180°C, 350°F, Gas Mark 4

1. Put the oil and the honey into a saucepan and
heat gently until the honey has melted. Remove
from the heat and stir in all the remaining
ingredients.
2. Press the mixture into a greased 28 × 18cm
(11 × 7 inch) baking tin and level the top.
3. Bake in a preheated oven for 20–25 minutes
until the biscuit is golden brown. Mark it into
bars while it is still hot. Cool slightly, then cut
into bars. Remove them from the tin and cool
on a wire rack.

Makes 16

Nutrition content per serving   Carbohydrate: 17g   Fat: 8g
Fibre: 2g   Kilocalories: 144

COCONUT-OAT CHEWS

75g (3oz) plain flour
100g (4oz) caster sugar
50g (2oz) desiccated coconut
50g (2oz) porridge oats
25g (1oz) shelled walnuts, chopped
1 teaspoon bicarbonate of soda
2 tablespoons golden syrup
100g (4oz) butter
3 tablespoons water

Preparation time: 10 minutes
Cooking time: 12–15 minutes
Oven: 180°C, 350°F, Gas Mark 4

1. Mix together the flour, sugar, coconut, oats,
walnuts and bicarbonate of soda in a bowl.
2. Place the syrup and butter in a saucepan.
Heat until the butter has melted. Add the dry
ingredients and water to the pan and mix well.
3. Shape the mixture into balls about 2.5cm
(1 inch) across. Place a little apart on greased
baking sheets. Bake in a preheated oven for
12–15 minutes, until golden brown.
4. Leave on the baking sheets for 2 minutes,
then transfer to a wire rack to cool completely.

Makes about 25

Nutrition content per serving   Carbohydrate: 9g   Fat: 5g
Fibre: 1g   Kilocalories: 85

TOP: Florentine Slices; BOTTOM LEFT: Crunchy
Muesli Bars; BOTTOM RIGHT: Coconut-Oat Chews.

Biscuits

♦

& COOKIES

Biscuits and cookies are very easy to make and, if you aren't standing guard, are liable to be as quick to eat as they are to bake. It's easy to understand the popularity of biscuits and cookies – they are sweet, perfectly textured, and just the right size.

In this chapter you will find recipes for biscuits of all shapes and sizes, containing nuts, dried fruits, chocolate chips, oats, marmalade, peanut butter, and many other ingredients. Flavoured with coffee, cocoa, lemon, orange, ginger, and cinnamon, they range in texture from crisp to chewy to meltingly tender.

Hazelnut Tuiles; Ginger Shortbread
(see recipes on page 76).

HAZELNUT TUILES

50g (2oz) butter
2 egg whites
65g (2½oz) caster sugar
few drops of vanilla essence
50g (2oz) plain flour, sifted
50g (2oz) shelled hazelnuts, chopped
little icing sugar

Preparation time: 10 minutes
Cooking time: 5–6 minutes
Oven: 200°C, 400°F, Gas Mark 6

1. Melt the butter in a saucepan and leave to cool. Whisk the egg whites until thick and frothy. Add the sugar and beat again until thick and white. Add the vanilla essence to the butter. Fold the flour into the egg white mixture, about a third at a time, alternating with the melted butter. Fold in the chopped nuts.
2. Put teaspoons of the mixture on to greased and floured baking sheets, taking care to keep them widely spaced. Spread each one out to a thin 6cm (2½ inch) circle. Sift a little icing sugar over them. Place in a preheated oven and bake for 5–6 minutes until coloured around the edges.
3. Have a greased rolling pin ready for shaping the tuiles. Place each biscuit on the rolling pin and press it into a curve. This must be done while the biscuits are warm and pliable, as they come from the oven. After shaping, cool on a wire rack.

Makes 20

Nutrition content per serving   Carbohydrate: 6g   Fat: 3g
Fibre: 0g   Kilocalories: 54

GINGER SHORTBREAD

225g (8oz) butter, softened
100g (4oz) caster sugar
225g (8oz) plain flour
2 teaspoons ground ginger
caster sugar, for sprinkling

Preparation time: 20 minutes
Cooking time: 15–20 minutes
Oven: 160°C, 325°F, Gas Mark 3

1. Cream together the butter and sugar on a clean surface. Gradually work in the sifted flour and ginger to form a dough. Knead until smooth.
2. Roll out to 5 mm (¼ inch) thick and cut into rounds with a medium scone cutter, or any shaped cutter. Place on a baking sheet.
3. Bake in a preheated oven until golden brown, and sprinkle with caster sugar while still warm. Cool on a wire rack.

Makes about 36

Nutrition content per serving   Carbohydrate: 9g   Fat: 5g
Fibre: 0g   Kilocalories: 81

BRANDY SNAPS

100g (4oz) butter
100g (4oz) demerara sugar
125g (5oz) golden syrup
100g (4oz) plain flour
2 teaspoons ground ginger
whipped cream, to serve (optional)

Preparation time: 1½ hours, plus setting
Cooking time: 8 minutes per batch
Oven: 160°C, 325°F, Gas Mark 3

1. Put the butter, sugar and syrup into a saucepan and stir over a low heat until the sugar and butter have melted. Sift the flour and ginger together, add to the melted mixture and beat well until smooth.
2. Lightly grease a baking sheet and, allowing for spreading, place 1 teaspoon of mixture on the sheet. (You should be able to bake two biscuits per sheet.) Keep the remaining mixture warm. Bake in the centre of a preheated oven for 8 minutes or until pale gold.
3. Leave for 1 minute on the baking sheet, then remove with a palette knife and roll the brandy snap round the handle of a wooden spoon so that the smooth side is outermost. Leave for 2 minutes to set, then slide off and cool on a wire rack. Repeat the procedure with the rest of the mixture.
4. Serve plain or filled with whipped cream.

Makes about 36

Nutrition content per serving (plain)   Carbohydrate: 8g
Fat: 2g   Fibre: 0g   Kilocalories: 52

Brandy Snaps.

LANGUES DE CHATS

120ml (4fl oz) double cream
120g (4½oz) icing sugar, sifted
120g (4½oz) plain flour, sifted
2 egg whites
finely grated rind of 1 lemon

Preparation time: 20 minutes
Cooking time: 7–8 minutes
Oven: 190°C, 375°F, Gas Mark 5

1. Place the cream and icing sugar in a bowl and stir together. Add the flour and stir in lightly. Whisk the egg whites until stiff and standing in peaks. Fold a third of the egg white into the mixture at a time. Add the lemon rind and lightly mix until evenly blended.
2. Put into a piping bag fitted with a 5 mm (¼ inch) or 1cm (½ inch) plain nozzle and pipe in finger lengths on to a greased baking sheet.
3. As each baking sheet is filled, place in a preheated oven and bake for 7–8 minutes until the biscuits are golden brown round the edges, but still pale in the centre. Cool on a wire rack.

Makes 50 small or 20 large biscuits

Nutrition content per serving   Carbohydrate: 11 or 4g
Fat: 3 or 1g   Fibre: 0g   Kilocalories: 73 or 29

PINWHEELS

100g (4oz) unsalted butter
100g (4oz) vanilla sugar
1 teaspoon grated lemon rind
1 egg
200g (7oz) plain flour
50g (2oz) ground walnuts
½ teaspoon baking powder
pinch of salt
1 tablespoon cocoa powder

Preparation time: 20 minutes, plus chilling
Cooking time: 8–10 minutes
Oven: 200°C, 400°F, Gas Mark 6

1. Beat the butter in a mixing bowl until pale and soft. Add the sugar and lemon rind and beat until light and fluffy. Beat in the egg. Sift together the flour, walnuts, baking powder and salt into the bowl and fold into the butter mixture.
2. Halve the dough and set one half aside. Sift the cocoa powder into the bowl with the remaining dough and mix well.
3. Wrap each portion of dough in greaseproof paper and chill for 1 hour or until firm enough to roll.
4. Roll out each portion of dough into rectangles of equal size 5 mm (¼ inch) thick. Place one rectangle on top of the other and press gently to seal together. Trim away any uneven sides and roll up the dough from a long side like a Swiss roll. Wrap the roll in greaseproof paper and chill for 2 hours or until firm enough to slice.
5. Cut the dough into slices 8 mm (⅓ inch) thick and place on buttered baking sheets. Bake in a preheated oven for 8–10 minutes, until the edges are crisp. Remove to a wire rack to cool.

Makes 30

Nutrition content per serving   Carbohydrate: 9g   Fat: 4g
Fibre: 0g   Kilocalories: 74

CITRUS ALMOND GALETTES

65g (2½oz) butter, softened
90g (3½oz) caster sugar
75g (3oz) blanched almonds, chopped
75g (3oz) candied orange peel, chopped
40g (1½oz) plain flour, sifted
2 teaspoons milk

Preparation time: 15 minutes
Cooking time: 5–7 minutes
Oven: 220°C, 425°F, Gas Mark 7

1. Cream the butter and sugar together until light and fluffy. Stir in the almonds and orange peel, then the flour and milk.
2. Place the mixture in small spoonfuls 5cm (2 inches) apart on a lightly greased baking sheet. Flatten each spoonful gently with a wet fork.
3. Bake in a preheated oven for 5–7 minutes. Allow the biscuits to cool on the baking sheet for 3–4 minutes before removing to a wire rack.

Makes 18–20

Nutrition content per serving   Carbohydrate: 10–9g   Fat: 5g
Fibre: 1g   Kilocalories: 88–79

FROM TOP TO BOTTOM: Pinwheels; Langues de Chats; Citrus Almond Galettes.

ANISEED & SESAME SEED BISCUITS

250ml (8fl oz) olive oil
2 long strips lemon peel
1 tablespoon aniseed
1 tablespoon sesame seeds
5 tablespoons dry white wine
finely grated rind of ½ lemon
finely grated rind of ½ orange
50g (2oz) caster sugar
450g (1 lb) plain flour
2 teaspoons ground cinnamon
1 egg white, beaten
3 tablespoons nibbed or chopped blanched almonds

Preparation time: 30 minutes, plus standing and chilling
Cooking time: 23–28 minutes
Oven: 180°C, 350°F, Gas Mark 4

1. Heat the olive oil in a shallow frying pan over a moderate heat for 2–3 minutes. Remove from the heat and add the lemon peel, aniseed and sesame seeds. Leave to cool completely.
2. Remove the lemon peel and pour the oil and seeds into a large mixing bowl.
3. Stir in the white wine, lemon and orange rind and caster sugar.
4. Sift together the flour and cinnamon and beat, little by little, into the wine and oil mixture. If the mixture becomes very stiff, work the dough with your hands.
5. When the dough is smooth, shape it into a neat ball, wrap it in cling film and chill for 30 minutes.
6. Divide the dough into 16 pieces and shape each one by hand into a round flat biscuit.
7. Place the biscuits on lightly greased baking sheets, allowing plenty of room for spreading.
8. Brush the tops of the biscuits with beaten egg white and press a few almond pieces into each one.
9. Place in a preheated oven and bake for 20–25 minutes.
10. Cool on a wire rack.

Makes about 16

Nutrition content per serving   Carbohydrate: 26g   Fat: 18g
Fibre: 1g   Kilocalories: 276

COFFEE KISSES

100g (4oz) butter, softened
50g (2oz) caster sugar
125g (5oz) self-raising flour
3 tablespoons strong black coffee
icing sugar, for dusting
ICING:
50g (2oz) butter, softened
100g (4oz) icing sugar, sifted
1 tablespoon strong black coffee

Preparation time: 20 minutes
Cooking time: 10 minutes
Oven: 190°C, 375°F, Gas Mark 5

1. Place the butter and sugar in a bowl. Beat with a wooden spoon for 10 minutes, or in a mixer for 5 minutes, until light and fluffy.
2. Add the flour and coffee and mix to a stiff dough. Place in a piping bag fitted with a large star tube. Pipe an even number of small stars of the mixture, a little apart, on a greased baking sheet. The mixture will make about 30 stars.
3. Bake in a preheated oven for 10 minutes, until just beginning to colour. Cool on the baking sheet for 5 minutes, then remove and leave to cool completely on a wire rack.
4. To make the icing, beat together the butter, icing sugar and coffee until light and creamy.
5. Sandwich pairs of stars together with a little icing, then dust with icing sugar.

Makes about 15

Nutrition content per serving   Carbohydrate: 11g   Fat: 6g
Fibre: 0g   Kilocalories: 95

ABOVE: Coffee Kisses.
RIGHT: Aniseed & Sesame Seed Biscuits.

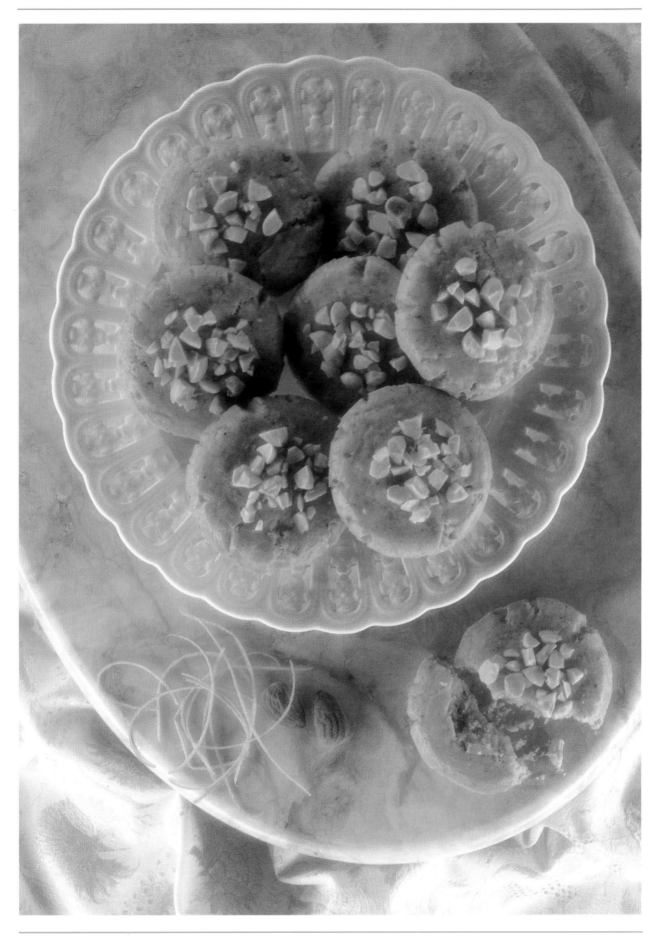

OAT CHOCOLATE CHIP COOKIES

100g (4oz) butter
100g (4oz) caster sugar
1 egg (size 1), beaten
½ teaspoon vanilla essence
75g (3oz) plain flour
pinch of salt
40g (1½oz) rolled oats
100g (4oz) chocolate chips

Preparation time: 20 minutes
Cooking time: 12–15 minutes
Oven: 180°C, 350°F, Gas Mark 4

1. Cream the butter and sugar together until light and fluffy. Gradually beat in the egg and vanilla essence. Sift in the flour and salt. Fold into the creamed mixture together with the oats and chocolate chips.
2. Put teaspoons of the mixture on to very well greased baking sheets; you will probably have to bake the biscuits in two batches. Bake in a preheated oven for 12–15 minutes or until very lightly browned.
3. Leave the cookies to cool on the baking sheets for a minute, then remove with a palette knife and cool completely on wire racks.

Makes about 36

Nutrition content per serving   Carbohydrate: 7g   Fat: 3g
Fibre: 0g   Kilocalories: 60

SPICED ORANGE BISCUITS

225g (8oz) plain flour
generous pinch of ground cinnamon
generous pinch of ground mixed spice
75g (3oz) caster sugar
150g (5oz) butter, softened
2 egg yolks
finely grated rind of 1 orange
½ teaspoon ground aniseed
75g (3oz) block plain chocolate, melted,
   to decorate

Preparation time: 25 minutes, plus chilling
Cooking time: 10–12 minutes
Oven: 190°C, 375°F, Gas Mark 5

1. Sift the flour, cinnamon and mixed spice into a bowl. Add the caster sugar, butter, egg yolks, orange rind and aniseed, and work to a smooth dough – you will find this easier to do by hand. Wrap in foil or cling film and chill for 1 hour.
2. Using a large piping bag fitted with a large star nozzle, pipe 10cm (4 inch) lengths on lightly greased baking sheets. Place in a preheated oven and bake for 10–12 minutes until lightly golden. Remove the biscuits to a wire rack and allow to cool.
3. Dip one end of each biscuit into the melted chocolate. Place on a sheet of greased greaseproof paper until the chocolate has set.

Makes about 20

Nutrition content per serving   Carbohydrate: 15g   Fat: 8g
Fibre: 0g   Kilocalories: 136

CARROT & MARMALADE COOKIES

100g (4oz) butter, softened
100g (4oz) caster sugar
1 egg, beaten
4 tablespoons coarse-cut marmalade
2 medium carrots, peeled and grated
200g (7oz) plain flour
½ teaspoon salt
½ teaspoon baking powder
finely grated rind of 1 orange
75g (3oz) raisins, chopped

Preparation time: about 20 minutes
Cooking time: 12–15 minutes
Oven: 180°C, 350°F, Gas Mark 4

1. Place the butter and sugar in a bowl and beat until light and fluffy. Add the beaten egg.
2. Beat in the marmalade and grated carrots.
3. Sift the flour, salt and baking powder together and stir into the creamed mixture, together with the orange rind and raisins.
4. Place teaspoons of the mixture on to lightly greased baking sheets, allowing room for spreading.
5. Place in a preheated oven and bake for 12–15 minutes until lightly golden. Leave to cool on a wire rack.

Makes about 24

Nutrition content per serving   Carbohydrate: 15g   Fat: 4g
Fibre: 1g   Kilocalories: 95

FROM TOP TO BOTTOM: Oat Chocolate Chip Cookies; Spiced Orange Biscuits; Carrot & Marmalade Cookies.

ROCK CAKES

50ml (2fl oz) boiling water
150g (5oz) sultanas or raisins
50g (2oz) butter, softened
90g (3½oz) soft dark brown sugar
1 egg
25g (1oz) shelled walnuts or hazelnuts, chopped
150g (5oz) plain flour
½ teaspoon baking powder
½ teaspoon salt
½ teaspoon ground cinnamon

Preparation time: about 8 minutes
Cooking time: about 20 minutes
Oven: 180°C, 350°F, Gas Mark 4

1. Pour the boiling water over the sultanas or raisins and set aside. Cream together the butter and sugar and beat in the egg.
2. Stir in the nuts. Sift the dry ingredients together and stir into the mixture. Finally, stir in the sultanas and their liquid and beat well.
3. Drop the mixture by heaped teaspoonfuls, spaced about 4cm (1½ inches) apart, on to lightly greased baking sheets. Bake in a preheated oven for 15–20 minutes until just firm.
4. Remove from the baking sheets while still warm and cool on a wire rack.

Makes about 20

Nutrition content per serving   Carbohydrate: 16g   Fat: 3g
Fibre: 1g   Kilocalories: 92

SPONGE FINGER BISCUITS

3 eggs, separated
75g (3oz) caster sugar
90g (3½oz) plain flour, sifted
2 drops vanilla essence
icing sugar, sifted

Preparation time: 30 minutes
Cooking time: 10–12 minutes
Oven: 180°C, 350°F, Gas Mark 4

1. Line two baking sheets with lightly greased greaseproof paper and set aside.
2. Place the egg yolks and sugar in a bowl and beat together until thick and pale in colour.
3. Beat the egg whites until stiff and fold into the yolk mixture together with the sifted flour and vanilla essence. Spoon the mixture into a piping bag fitted with a 1cm (½ inch) plain nozzle. Pipe into finger lengths on the greaseproof paper.
4. Dust with sifted icing sugar and bake in a preheated oven for 10–12 minutes. When cooked, carefully remove from the paper and allow the biscuits to cool on a wire rack.

Variation: When cold, the ends of the biscuits may be dipped in melted chocolate.

Makes 20

Nutrition content per serving   Carbohydrate: 8g   Fat: 1g
Fibre: 0g   Kilocalories: 45

COCOA WAFERS

100g (4oz) unsalted butter
175g (6oz) caster sugar
1 egg yolk
1 tablespoon strong black coffee
50g (2oz) cocoa powder
100g (4oz) plain flour
1 teaspoon baking powder
pinch of salt

Preparation time: 15 minutes, plus chilling
Cooking time: 8–10 minutes per batch
Oven: 200°C, 400°F, Gas Mark 6

1. Beat the butter in a mixing bowl until pale and soft. Add 150g (5oz) of the sugar and beat together until light and fluffy. Beat in the egg yolk and coffee and mix well. Sift the cocoa powder, flour, baking powder and salt into the bowl and mix in until just incorporated.
2. Shape the dough into a roll 6cm (2½ inches) in diameter. Wrap the roll in greaseproof paper and chill for 2 hours or until firm.
3. Cut the dough into slices 3mm (⅛ inch) thick and place on ungreased baking sheets. Lightly sprinkle each 'wafer' with some of the remaining sugar, pressing it in gently.
4. Bake in a preheated oven for 6–8 minutes, until the outside just darkens. Remove to a wire rack to cool.

Makes about 40

Nutrition content per serving   Carbohydrate: 7g   Fat: 3g
Fibre: 0g   Kilocalories: 50

FROM TOP TO BOTTOM: Rock Cakes; Sponge Finger Biscuits; Cocoa Wafers.

PEANUT BISCUITS

275g (10oz) plain flour
½ teaspoon baking powder
½ teaspoon salt
½ teaspoon bicarbonate of soda
100g (4oz) butter
225g (8oz) soft light brown sugar
100g (4oz) crunchy peanut butter
2 eggs, beaten

Preparation time: 15 minutes
Cooking time: 12–15 minutes
Oven: 200°C, 400°F, Gas Mark 6

1. Sift the flour, baking powder, salt and bicarbonate of soda into a bowl. Add the butter, cut into pieces, and rub into the flour until the mixture resembles fine breadcrumbs.
2. Stir in the sugar. Add the peanut butter and beaten eggs and mix to a soft dough.
3. Form the dough into small balls, about 2.5cm (1 inch) across, and place a little apart on greased baking sheets. Mark each biscuit by pressing the surface with a fork to make a criss-cross pattern.
4. Bake in a preheated oven for 12–15 minutes until risen. Remove and leave for 1 minute, then transfer to a wire rack to cool.

Makes about 50

Nutrition content per serving   Carbohydrate: 9g   Fat: 3g
Fibre: 0g   Kilocalories: 67

SPICED SULTANA BISCUITS

225g (8oz) self-raising flour
1 teaspoon ground mixed spice
pinch of salt
100g (4oz) wholemeal flour
100g (4oz) demerara sugar
150g (5oz) butter
1 egg, beaten
50g (2oz) sultanas
a little extra demerara sugar, for sprinkling

Preparation time: 30 minutes, plus chilling
Cooking time: 10–12 minutes
Oven: 180°C, 350°F, Gas Mark 4

1. Sift the self-raising flour, spice and salt into a bowl. Stir in the wholemeal flour and the sugar. Rub in the butter with the fingertips, then stir in the egg to give a stiff dough.
2. Turn the dough out on to a floured surface and work in the sultanas with the fingertips until evenly distributed throughout the dough. Sprinkle with more flour if the dough becomes too sticky. Form into a ball, wrap in foil and chill for at least 30 minutes until firm.
3. Roll out small pieces of the dough on a floured surface and cut into rounds using a 5cm (2 inch) fluted biscuit cutter. Sprinkle the dough and surface with flour while rolling and cutting as the dough is rich and sticky.
4. Place on baking sheets, prick all over with a fork and sprinkle with demerara sugar. Bake in a preheated oven for 10–12 minutes until golden brown and set. Transfer immediately to a wire rack and leave to cool.

Makes 30–35

Nutrition content per serving   Carbohydrate: 13–11g   Fat: 4g
Fibre: 1g   Kilocalories: 95–81

MACAROONS

100g (4oz) ground almonds
100g (4oz) caster sugar
2 egg whites
¼ teaspoon almond essence
rice paper, for lining
10 shelled almonds

Preparation time: 10 minutes
Cooking time: 20–25 minutes
Oven: 180°C, 350°F, Gas Mark 4

1. Mix together the ground almonds and sugar.
2. Whisk the egg whites until stiff. Fold the almond mixture and essence into the egg whites.
3. Place the mixture in a piping bag fitted with a large plain tube. Pipe 10 rounds about 5cm (2 inches) across on to a baking sheet lined with rice paper. Press an almond into the centre of each.
4. Bake in a preheated oven for 20–25 minutes, until lightly browned and firm. Remove and cool on a wire rack, then trim off the extra rice paper.

Makes 10

Nutrition content per serving   Carbohydrate: 11g   Fat: 6g
Fibre: 2g   Kilocalories: 110

TOP LEFT: Peanut Biscuits; TOP RIGHT: Spiced Sultana Biscuits; BOTTOM: Macaroons:

GINGER SNAPS

75g (3oz) butter
75g (3oz) dark soft brown sugar
2 tablespoons golden syrup
2 tablespoons black treacle
150g (6oz) self-raising flour
2 teaspoons ground ginger

Preparation time: 15 minutes
Cooking time: 7–10 minutes
Oven: 180°C, 350°F, Gas Mark 4

1. Put the butter, sugar, syrup and treacle in a pan and heat gently until melted, stirring occasionally. Sift the flour and ginger into a bowl, then stir in the melted mixture until the dough draws together.
2. Put teaspoonfuls of the mixture on lightly greased baking sheets, spacing them well apart. Press down with the fingertips to form flat round shapes. Bake in a preheated oven for 7–10 minutes.
3. Leave to set on the baking sheets for a few minutes, then transfer to a wire rack and leave to cool completely. Wrap neatly in foil and store in an airtight container.

Makes about 30

Nutrition content per serving   Carbohydrate: 8g   Fat: 2g
Fibre: 0g   Kilocalories: 52

DEMERARA BISCUITS

225g (8oz) plain flour
pinch of salt
175g (6oz) butter
150g (5oz) demerara sugar

Preparation time: 30 minutes, plus chilling
Cooking time: 20 minutes
Oven: 160°C, 325°F, Gas Mark 3

1. Sift the flour and salt into a bowl. Cream the butter until soft and then add 100g (4oz) of the sugar and beat until light and fluffy. Blend in the flour and work until smooth.
2. Divide the mixture into two equal pieces and roll out each to form a sausage 15cm (6 inches) long. Roll in the remaining sugar, then wrap in foil and chill in the refrigerator until firm.
3. Cut each sausage into 16 slices and place on greased baking sheets. Bake in a preheated oven

for 20 minutes, or until the biscuits are pale golden brown at the edges. Leave to cool on a wire rack.

Makes 32

Nutrition content per serving   Carbohydrate: 11g   Fat: 5g
Fibre: 0g   Kilocalories: 84

ORANGE REFRIGERATOR COOKIES

The dough for these cookies can be kept in the refrigerator, well wrapped, for a week. Simply slice off as many biscuits as you require.

275g (10oz) plain flour
1 teaspoon baking powder
150g (5oz) butter, softened
175g (6oz) caster sugar
2 teaspoons finely grated orange rind
1 egg (size 1), lightly beaten
50g (2oz) currants
extra caster sugar, for dusting

Preparation time: 25 minutes, plus chilling
Cooking time: about 15 minutes
Oven: 180°C, 350°F, Gas Mark 4

1. Sift together the flour and baking powder. Cream the butter, sugar and orange rind together until light and fluffy. Beat in the egg. Stir in the currants and the flour until the mixture clings together.
2. Turn on to a lightly floured surface and form with your hands into a sausage shape about 5cm (2 inches) in diameter. Wrap in foil or greaseproof paper and chill in the refrigerator for at least 2 hours.
3. To cook the biscuits, thinly slice off as many as you need and place on greased baking sheets. Sprinkle with sugar and bake in a preheated oven for about 15 minutes. Cool on the sheets for 2 minutes, then transfer to a wire rack.

Makes about 48

Nutrition content per serving   Carbohydrate: 9g   Fat: 3g
Fibre: 0g   Kilocalories: 63

TOP LEFT: Ginger Snaps; TOP RIGHT: Demerara Biscuits; BOTTOM: Orange Refrigerator Biscuits.

No-bake cakes

◆

& BISCUITS

It's fun to make cakes and biscuits that don't have
to be baked. Most of the recipes here are very
easy, and children will enjoy trying them.
There's a cake based on crushed biscuits and
ground almonds, flavoured with coffee and cocoa
and covered with melted chocolate. Another cake
layers a rich chestnut and chocolate mixture with
finger biscuits and is iced with whipped cream.
The cheesecake has a wonderful filling of custard,
curd cheese, cream and pineapple set with
gelatine, and is finished with a layer of
soured cream.
Bars are made with dried fruits and nuts bound
together with honey, and with coconut, glacé
cherries, sultanas and crushed biscuits set in a
chocolate fudge.

Pineapple Cheesecake (see recipe on page 93).

CHOCOLATE REFRIGERATOR CAKE

100g (4oz) plain chocolate, broken into small
  pieces
100g (4oz) unsalted butter, softened
50g (2oz) icing sugar, sifted
225g (8oz) unsweetened chestnut purée
300ml ($\frac{1}{2}$ pint) double or whipping cream, whipped
  to form soft peaks
20–25 plain finger biscuits
4–5 tablespoons brandy or rum, or to taste
grated chocolate, to decorate (optional)

Preparation time: 20 minutes, plus chilling

1. Line a 20 × 10cm (8 × 4 inch) loaf tin with a sheet of cling film.
2. Place the chocolate in a bowl and melt over a pan of hot water. Allow to cool.
3. Cream the butter and sugar together until light and fluffy. Beat in the chocolate and chestnut purée until the mixture is smooth. Stir in 2 tablespoons of the cream, then cover the remainder and refrigerate until later.
4. Arrange a row of biscuits in the base of the prepared tin. Sprinkle a little brandy or rum over and cover with a layer of the chestnut mixture. Repeat the layers, ending with a layer of biscuits.
5. Cover with a piece of greaseproof paper or cling film. Place a light weight on top and refrigerate for 3–4 hours or overnight.
6. Turn out on to a serving dish. Remove the cling film. Whip the remaining cream, if necessary, until it is a little stiffer than soft peak and spread over the top and sides of the refrigerator cake. Fluff up like snow icing. If desired, sprinkle a little grated chocolate over the top. Refrigerate until required.

Serves 6–8

Nutrition content per serving   Carbohydrate: 65–49g
Fat: 52–39g   Fibre: 4–3g   Kilocalories: 767–575

PINEAPPLE CHEESECAKE

2 tablespoons powdered gelatine
175g (6oz) sugar
pinch of salt
3 eggs, separated
300ml ($\frac{1}{2}$ pint) milk
1 × 225g (8oz) can crushed pineapple in natural
  juice
550g (1$\frac{1}{4}$ lb) curd cheese
2 teaspoons grated lemon rind
3 tablespoons lemon juice
300ml ($\frac{1}{2}$ pint) double cream
BASE:
100g (4oz) butter, melted
225g (8oz) digestive biscuits, finely crushed
TO DECORATE:
150ml ($\frac{1}{4}$ pint) soured cream
candied pineapple
flaked almonds, toasted

Preparation time: 50 minutes, plus chilling
Cooking time: about 15 minutes

1. First make the base. Mix the melted butter with the biscuit crumbs and press evenly over the bottom of a greased 24cm (9$\frac{1}{2}$ inch) springform tin. Chill while you make the filling.
2. In a heatproof mixing bowl, mix together the gelatine, sugar and salt.
3. With a fork, lightly beat the egg yolks with the milk and add to the sugar mixture. Mix in the crushed pineapple.
4. Set the mixing bowl over a pan of simmering water and stir for about 15 minutes until the mixture starts to thicken. Draw off the heat and pour into a large mixing bowl. Set aside to cool.
5. Beat together the curd cheese, lemon rind and lemon juice. Gradually add the cooled pineapple mixture and combine well. Set aside until almost on the point of setting.
6. Whisk the egg whites until stiff. Whip the double cream until stiff. Fold alternate spoonfuls of whipped cream and egg white into the cheese mixture. Pour into the tin and carefully smooth over. Chill for 5 hours.
7. To serve, carefully remove the sides of the tin and set the cheesecake on a serving plate. Gently smooth the soured cream over the surface and decorate with the candied pineapple and toasted almond flakes.

Serves 12

Nutrition content per serving   Carbohydrate: 24g   Fat: 30g
Fibre: 1g   Kilocalories: 411

Chocolate Refrigerator Cake.

ITALIAN MOCHA CAKE

150g (5oz) butter, softened
1 tablespoon caster sugar
1 tablespoon golden syrup
2 tablespoons cocoa powder
250g (9oz) digestive biscuits, finely crushed
25g (1oz) ground almonds
2 teaspoons coffee essence
75g (3oz) plain chocolate

Preparation time: 30 minutes, plus chilling

1. Grease a shallow 20cm (8 inch) square tin.
2. Cream the butter and sugar together until pale and fluffy. Place the syrup in a saucepan and warm gently over a low heat. Remove from the heat and add the cocoa, biscuit crumbs, almonds and coffee essence. Allow to cool and stir into the creamed mixture.
3. Press the mixture into the prepared tin. Cover and chill until firm.
4. To finish, melt the chocolate, pour evenly over the cake and leave to set.

Serves 4

Nutrition content per serving   Carbohydrate: 63g   Fat: 54g
Fibre: 4g   Kilocalories: 760

FRUITY BARS

175g (6oz) best quality dried apricots, finely
*   chopped*
50g (2oz) seedless raisins, finely chopped
50g (2oz) shelled pecan nuts, finely chopped
50g (2oz) ground hazelnuts
grated rind of 1 orange
4 teaspoons clear honey
about 4 teaspoons lemon juice
icing sugar, for dusting

Preparation time: 15 minutes, plus chilling

1. Combine the apricots, raisins, pecan nuts, hazelnuts and orange rind in a small bowl.
2. Mix in all the honey and 2 teaspoons of the lemon juice. Stir in the remaining juice gradually until the mixture is a firm paste.
3. Turn the mixture on to a piece of foil and pat into an oblong shape about 2cm ($\frac{3}{4}$ inch) thick.
4. Wrap the foil round to make a flat packet and refrigerate for about 3 hours until firm.
5. Remove the foil and cut the fruit and nut cake with a sharp knife into small bars about

7.5cm (3 inches) long and 4cm ($1\frac{1}{2}$ inches) wide, or smaller if to be served as petits fours.
6. Dust lightly with icing sugar before serving.

Makes about 8

Nutrition content per serving   Carbohydrate: 20g   Fat: 5g
Fibre: 6g   Kilocalories: 134

CHOCOLATE FUDGE BARS

4 tablespoons golden syrup
100g (4oz) butter
100g (4oz) plain chocolate, broken into pieces
225g (8oz) digestive or other unfilled or coated
*   sweet biscuits, coarsely crushed*
50g (2oz) desiccated coconut or chopped nuts
50g (2oz) glacé cherries, quartered
50g (2oz) sultanas

Preparation time: about 15 minutes, plus chilling

1. Spoon the syrup into a heavy-based saucepan and add the butter. Heat gently until both are melted and stir well.
2. Away from the heat, add the chocolate and stir vigorously until melted.
3. Stir the biscuit crumbs, coconut or nuts, cherries and sultanas into the chocolate mixture. Mix well.
4. Line the base of an 18cm (7 inch) square cake tin with greased greaseproof paper. Pour in the mixture, spread evenly and press down firmly. Cool, then chill until set, about 3 hours.
5. Carefully turn out the biscuit slab on to a chopping board and cut into bars. Keep chilled in warm weather.

Makes 15–20

Nutrition content per serving   Carbohydrate: 22–16g
Fat: 13–9g   Fibre: 2–1g   Kilocalories: 202–152

FROM TOP TO BOTTOM: Italian Mocha Cake; Fruity Bars; Chocolate Fudge Bars.

INDEX